Mustine Hearst

Stan Lavitt

The Horses of San Simeon

The Horses of San Simeon

BY MRS. WILLIAM RANDOLPH HEARST, JR.

PAINTINGS AND DRAWINGS BY SAM SAVITT

PHOTOGRAPHS BY ALIX COLEMAN

FOREWORD BY ALEXANDER MACKAY-SMITH

San Simeon Press / San Simeon, California

Library of Congress Cataloging in Publication Data
Hearst, William Randolph, Mrs.
    The horses of San Simeon.
    Bibliography, p.
    1. Horses—California—San Simeon Region—History.
    2. San Simeon Ranch (Calif.)—History. 3. Hearst family.
    I. Title.
SF284.U5H43   1985   636.1'009794'78   85-14264

Barbara Burn, Editor
Michael Shroyer, Designer
Typographic Images, Typesetter
Princeton Polychrome, Printer

To my favorite men:
my husband, Will,
my sons, Will and Austin,
and my grandson, Willie.
My heart treasures the many
precious hours we have spent together
at San Simeon.

Contents

Foreword *Alexander Mackay-Smith*

*I*t is indeed fortunate that the Hearst family's love of horses and of the San Simeon ranch is being carried on by the third, fourth, and now fifth generation. It is also fortunate for the history of San Simeon that William Randolph Hearst, Jr., married a woman who shares these enthusiasms. Born in Warrenton, Virginia, Austine McDonnell Hearst was brought up in fox-hunting country and now serves as Joint Master of the Golden's Bridge Hunt at North Salem, New York, where she rides Arabian horses bred at San Simeon.

California's most famous ranch is a private kingdom of 79,000 acres, a vast unspoiled paradise of mountains, meadows, and valleys, which sweeps for miles along the beaches and rocks of the coastline. "The precipitous Santa Lucia Mountains, threaded with silver streams, open up to green valleys. On one side of the mountains the streams stumble west over rocks down to the sea, and on the other side the streams flow East into the broad, fertile Salinas River Valley.... The tides and fogs still come and go rhythmically, while the Santa Lucia Mountains stand untouched behind meadows that go rolling down to the ocean, flung like a white-fringed shawl on the beach."

These poetic words have been garnered from the prologue of Austine McDonnell Hearst's beautiful and absorbing book. Her ten years as the author of a nationally syndicated newspaper column, her Virginia background and upbringing, and her love of history of the land as well as horses combine to make her especially qualified to research and write this truly unique volume.

The San Simeon kingdom remains unspoiled because, for over a hundred years, it has been owned by a family which has loved the land and is determined, as much as is now possible, to keep it as it was when peopled by the Chumash Indians. It is in fact two kingdoms, east and west, divided by the Santa Lucia mountains, two different landscapes, two different climates.

The first Europeans to settle San Simeon were Spaniards, led by Father Junipero Serra and other Franciscans, who constructed mission churches, dwelling houses, and farm buildings on the cultivated farmlands of the fertile Salinas River valley beyond the mountains: San Antonio de Padua in 1771, San Miguel Arcángel in 1797. These missions established livestock ranches along the coast—San Simeon, Santa Rosa, and Piedra Blanca—where they grazed cattle, sheep, and horses on the rich native grasses. Under the management of their successors, the

Mexican dons, many of them absentee owners, the numbers of grazing sheep and cattle gradually diminished.

Using his newly acquired riches from mining, George Hearst began to reassemble the coastal ranches; it was in 1865 that he purchased his first parcel. This was land that had never before been abused or eroded either by cultivation or by overgrazing. Today, watching the fat cattle and the lovely Arabian horses in the pastures of San Simeon, it is thrilling to realize that these native grasses grow unchanged since the days of the Indians who migrated to these shores seven thousand years ago.

In addition to grasses suitable for livestock, the coastal ranches had other natural assets. Of prime importance were the never-failing streams of pure water from the mountains. Along these streams grew quantities of valuable timber; San Simeon today has one of the three surviving original stands of Monterey pines.

San Simeon's deep-water harbor and shelving beach provided constant communication with the outside world. Passing ships took on water and provisions and bought the sheep, cattle, and especially the horses that the *padres* had for sale. Russian merchants traded for sea otter pelts and sealskins. Whalers beached their catch, flensed the blubber, and boiled it in huge copper kettles to extract the oil. There was a constant supply of fish which Indian runners, using time-worn trails over the Santa Lucia Mountains, delivered fresh to the missions in the Salinas Valley.

The Franciscan fathers brought to the coastal ranches additional assets in the form of livestock. Even more important than sheep and cattle were their Andalusian horses from southern Spain. The exquisite horses of the Bedouin sheiks were ridden to North Africa by the invading Arabs where their bloodlines were mingled with those of the native Barbs. Successive invasions of Arabs and Moors brought these horses to the Iberian peninsula, where Celtic strains were added to the mixture, notably the pacing horses of Asturia and Galicia in northwest Spain. Thus evolved the strain known as the Andalusian, imported to the West Indies on his second voyage by Christopher Columbus in 1493 and to the North American continent (Mexico) by Cortés in 1519. Mexican dons rode them in parades and in bullfights at their fiestas. Today in Spain and Portugal they continue to be used for bullfighting on horseback. They are esteemed worldwide for their excellence in dressage display and competition.

George Hearst used cowponies of Quarter Horse type to work his cattle, but his passion was racing. Much of his success in various mining ventures stemmed from his ability to select able partners and lieutenants. Unlike many self-made men before and since, Hearst followed this same practice when building up his stable of Thoroughbred racehorses and when selecting breeding stock for his Piedra Blanca stud farm at San Simeon. During the winter of 1887–88, when service as one of California's United States Senators required him to spend much of his time in Washington, Hearst began to assemble a stable to race at Eastern tracks and breeding stock to provide replacements. He sought and obtained the advice of California's leading owners and breeders and purchased many of their horses—Theodore Winters, Lucky Baldwin, James Ben Ali Haggin, and Leland Stanford. When his first trainer Matt (Kid Glove) Allen proved unsatisfactory after a year and a half, Hearst did not hesitate to replace him with the successful black trainer, Albert Cooper, although it was mid-summer, in the middle of the racing season. Mrs. Hearst's book includes two absorbing chapters on George Hearst's racing and breeding activities, starring his great horse TOURNAMENT, leading money winner of 1890, and REY EL SANTA ANITA, conceived at Piedra Blanca, by imported *CHEVIOT, and winner in 1894 of the American Derby at Chicago for Lucky Baldwin.

George Hearst's unfortunate death in February 1891 brought to a close these promising beginnings. Hearst's great success as a breeder, for which he consequently never received credit, was largely reaped by purchasers at the dispersal sale.

His only child, William Randolph Hearst, who built a world-famous newspaper empire, inherited the immense family fortune on the death of his mother in 1919. W. R. Hearst was a connoisseur of the fine arts. The Spanish Baroque castle he built at San Simeon, filled with furniture, silver, tapestries, paintings, and sculpture of the period, was given after his death in 1951 to California, where it is now the state's number-one tourist attraction.

Hearst was also a connoisseur of horses. He loved to ride long distances through the Santa Lucia Mountains. As a political observer and a producer of motion pictures, he loved to entertain at his castle the many political figures, editors, actors, and producers who were his friends, and to take them on riding picnics. He liked beauty and color, not only in his surroundings, but also in his horses. In 1945, he organized an expedition to the Near East to purchase Arabian horses. Before that, he had crossed Arabian with Morgan mares to produce a new breed. He purchased and bred such color breeds as Palominos and Appaloosas to use as his personal mounts.

Collectors and readers will find themselves fortunate to own this book—those who love horses for their own sake; those with special interests in the many breeds brought to San Simeon and in their performance records; those who cherish the history of early California, of gold and silver mining, and of the Old West; those who appreciate the continuity of more than a century of ownership by a multitalented family; and those who enjoy its beautiful illustrations.

To Austine Hearst, many, many thanks for this fascinating and very special book.

San Simeon History: A Chronology

180 Million Years Ago—California and San Simeon under the sea.

20 Million Years Ago—Land Rises. Later, first horses develop on continent of North America, and cross over land bridges to Siberia and Asia. Become extinct in Americas.

7,000 Years Ago—Humans cross land bridges to North America.

1492—Columbus looking for China and India, discovers the New World for Spain, misnames the Indians.

1494—Columbus on second voyage brings horses to New World to Haiti.

1510—Twenty years after Columbus, book mentions an "island" called California. Maps thereafter show California as an island.

1519—Hernando Cortés lands eleven stallions, five mares on east coast of Mexico, thus restoring horses to American continent and completing the horse's journey around the world.

1542—Juan Rodriguez Cabrillo visits San Simeon, sailing his caravel to chart California's coast. Describes San Simeon, *Piedra Blanca*, "white rocks"; names harbor of Monterey "Bay of Pines."

1566—Returning to New Spain (Mexico) from the Philippines, Spanish galleons heading for Acapulco on Mexico's west coast regularly pass San Simeon.

1579—Sir Francis Drake, England's privateer, sails past San Simeon, hoping to capture Spanish galleons along California's coast.

1602—Sebastian Vizcaino, explorer, searches for safe ports for Spain. Lands, renames Cabrillo's Bay of Pines after Count of Monterey. Recommends a colony.

1603—More interested in riches from Mexico, Peru, and Manila, the Spanish Crown shelves the idea of colonies.

1769—Fearing that Russia or possibly England might claim Alta (upper) California, King Carlos III of Spain orders Governor General of New Spain to organize expeditions to explore and colonize region. Four expeditions start north, two by ship, two by land. Gaspar de Portola, head of one group, camps at San Simeon. Father Junipero Serra founds first two missions at San Diego and Monterey.

1771—Father Serra builds third mission, San Antonio de Padua. Famous for its horses, the mission claims Piedra Blanca as part of its holdings.

1773—Boundary established by Spain divides Alta California from Baja California. Later this line will divide Mexico from the United States.

1797—The 16th mission, San Miguel Arcángel, started by Father Lasuen with coastal acreage, San Simeon and Santa Rosa ranches, portions of today's Hearst ranch.

1810—Corrals built at San Simeon to hold horses and cattle of mission San Miguel.

1812—Russian American Company establishes outpost at Fort Ross to hunt sea otter, provide supplies to Russia's Alaska outposts. Later sold to John A. Sutter, Swiss pioneer, who received large grant subsequently.

1820—George Hearst born in Missouri. Monroe elected president.

1821—Mexico wins independence from Spain.

1822—California now a province of Mexico.

1833—Secularization deprives church missions of all lands, livestock, and buildings.

1835—Mexican Congress declares Los Angeles capital of California.

1836—Northern provinces ignore edict, recognize Monterey as capital.

1840—Don José Jesus de Pico sent to administer property of Mission San Antonio, receives grant of mission lands, Rancho Piedra Blanca.

1841—Mission San Miguel's property, Rancho Santa Rosa, granted to Julian Estrada.

1842—More San Miguel property, Rancho San Simeon, granted to José Ramon Estrada, brother of Julian.

1846—United States flag at last raised over Monterey; Mexican rule ended and California taken by United States. William Hearst, father of George, dies in Missouri.

1848—Treaty of Hidalgo ending war between United States and Mexico. Gold found by James W. Marshall at John A. Sutter's sawmill near Sacramento.

1849—Thousands of gold seekers start for California.

1850—California joins the Union. George Hearst rides from Missouri to California.

1852—Whaling station operates at San Simeon.

1858—Butterfield Overland Stage promises passage from Missouri to California, 2800 miles.

1860—Pony Express riders link Sacramento, California, to railroads at St. Joseph, Missouri.

1862—Gold from California mines helps United States in Civil War. George Hearst returns as millionaire to Missouri to marry Phoebe Apperson.

1863—George Hearst invests in racetrack at San Francisco. Birth of only son, William Randolph Hearst.

1865—George Hearst begins buying land to raise horses at San Simeon.

1869—First transcontinental railroad opened.

1874—United States builds first California lighthouse at Piedra Blanca.

1878—George Hearst builds San Simeon warehouses. Buys more horses and starts winning races.

1887—William Randolph Hearst becomes publisher of his first newspaper, *The San Francisco Examiner.*

1891—Death of Senator George Hearst.

1899—William Randolph Hearst leads the fight to force Spain to give up Cuba, the last European foothold on this continent. Phoebe Hearst helps her son buy newspapers.

1903—W. R. Hearst marries Millicent Willson.

1908—Birth of William Randolph Hearst, Jr.

1919—Death of Phoebe Apperson Hearst. Her only heir, William Randolph Hearst, starts building castle and enlarges publishing enterprises.

1945—After World War II, William Randolph Hearst sends expedition to England, Syria, and Lebanon to purchase Arabian horses.

1949—One hundred years after Gold Rush, birth of William Randolph Hearst, III, great-grandson of Senator George Hearst.

1951—Death of William Randolph Hearst, who leaves five sons, George, William, John, twins Randolph and David, and many grandchildren to carry on communications empire.

1955—Hearst Castle, furnishings, art works, and one hundred acres of gardens presented to State of California to be shown to public.

1980—The fourth William Randolph Hearst born in California.

1984—Almost one hundred years after W. R. Hearst became publisher of San Francisco paper his grandson, W. R. Hearst III, takes same job.

1985—These first chapters are finished. But the story of San Simeon, the Hearsts, and their horses will go on.

Prologue/The San Simeon Cavalcade of Horses

*G*o as far as you can into the sunset, as far west across our country as the land will take you. Finally, at the Pacific Ocean on the coast of California, you will come to San Simeon. A country unto itself, a never-never land unconquered by this century's smoke, skyscrapers, and sidewalks, San Simeon is bounded by ageless mountains and by the unending sea. The sea and the land lie side by side like lovers, caressing each other.

Flown over by birds of the mountains, of the plains, of the sea and the shorelines, roamed over by native deer, coyotes, and mountain lions, by sheep from the Himalayas and Asian antelopes, San Simeon is an improbable Peaceable Kingdom where zebras from Africa graze contentedly with domestic cows and horses. A turreted castle crowning one of the hills looks out over miles and miles of open land.

How can one describe such a place? Fantastic? Exotic? Enchanted? No, mere words won't do, for this place has no counterpart on earth in real life. Perhaps in dreams. Timelessness, and if there is such a word, placelessness belong to this magic kingdom aswirl in fog. Veils of fog trail up the hills from the sea while higher in the sky a vulture coasts the clouds and is the first to welcome the sun rising in back of San Simeon.

The vulture's ancestors were circling above the same scene when Spanish explorers on horseback tracked up the coast of California over two hundred years ago. Before them a tribe of tall, bronzed Indians called the Chumash had fished and camped along the coast for seven thousand years. After the Indians came the Spanish missionaries, who were followed in turn by Mexican settlers, American homesteaders, miners, and ranchers. And today millions of tourists from many nations flash by in their cars. Each of these groups has changed the land a little, adding to it and taking away, but man's impact has not been too destructive in these hills and pastures. The tides and fogs still come and go rhythmically, while the Santa Lucia Mountains stand untouched behind meadows that go rolling down to the ocean, flung like a white-fringed shawl on the beach.

San Simeon's Zebras by Sam Savitt. William Randolph Hearst maintained at San Simeon one of the largest private collection of zoo animals in the world, including a herd of Burchell's zebras, descendants of which continue to roam the ranch's natural grasslands.

Up and down that beach, swept by wind and waves, jumbles of rocks and steep banks rise again to gentle pastures. The land slowly climbs up steep canyons from streambeds lined with live oaks, sycamores, and bay trees. Gradually the hills crest high, higher, to the territory of the hawks and vultures. The precipitous Santa Lucia Mountains, threaded with silver streams, open up to green valleys. On one side of the mountains the streams stumble west over rocks down to the sea, and on the other side the streams flow east into the broad, fertile Salinas River valley.

The area, in fact, has two entirely different climates—one is damp and cool along the shore, while the other is hot and desert-dry inland. Temperatures can vary enormously within a few miles: when it is 40°F. on the ocean, it may register 110°F. in the shade only a few miles away. Vastly different groups of plants and animals are supported in each climate. Pelicans, cormorants, and gulls fly over the ocean, and sandpipers scurry along the beach; farther away from the sea are multitudes of ducks, peregrine falcons and many other kinds of hawks, white-tailed kites, California quails, great blue herons, Anna's hummingbirds, horned owls, and towhees. As wondrous as the variety of birds are the many native wild plants, some of which exist nowhere else on earth and have Latin names such as *Ceanothus hearstorium*.

In the chaparral and coastal scrub you find manzanita, toyon, and sagebrush populated with various species of lizards, coast mule deer, and wood rats. By the streams such trees as willows, sycamores, California bays, and live oaks shelter beavers, black bears, raccoons, gophers, moles, and kit foxes. On the mountains and in their foothills mountain lions and bobcats prowl among mixed deciduous and evergreen forests. High and low places alike are roamed by ubiquitous coyotes and native deer. A few introduced animals remain from the ones brought in by W. R. Hearst—sanbar deer from Asia, Himalayan tahr goats, aoudad or wild sheep from northern Africa.

In autumn myriads of monarch butterflies decorate the air overhead, and in winter and spring jeweled hordes of wildflowers are thrown down on the earth. The principal reason that this land still blooms with wildflowers instead of being suffocated under concrete is that all seventy-nine thousand acres have been maintained for 120 years by four generations of a single family as a working ranch capable of supporting its own animals on native grass.

Larger than some countries—Andorra, Monaco, and Liechtenstein, for instance—the ranch of San Simeon has had only a few owners. Since the Indians and the mission fathers, the Mexicans and a few homesteaders, it has belonged for more than a century to the Hearst family.

It started with a love story—the love of one man for his horses. That man, George Hearst, used his gold, dug from the land, to purchase

EVOLUTION - The horse family provides one of the best examples of the how and why of evolution. Horses developed from more ancient forms of life and clearly demonstrate the way all living organisms evolve with successive generations. Everyone has some acquaintance with this beautiful animal and can find a fascination in the story of how he gradually changed from Eohippus to the horse we know today

Eocene Period - Approx. 60 to 40 million years B.C.

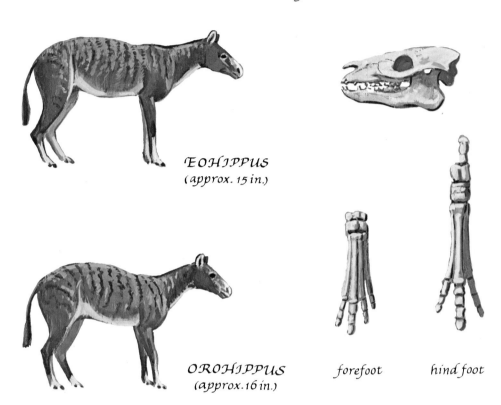

EOHIPPUS
(approx. 15 in.)

OROHIPPUS
(approx. 16 in.)

forefoot   hind foot

EOHIPPUS had a four-toed forefoot and a three-toed hind foot. He lived on leaves in a hot humid climate. As the temperature dropped the earth hardened and there was more grass, bringing a change in the teeth of OROHIPPUS.

Oligocene - Approx. 40 to 25 million years B.C.

MIOHIPPUS
(approx. 28 in.)

The Evolution of the Horse
by Sam Savitt

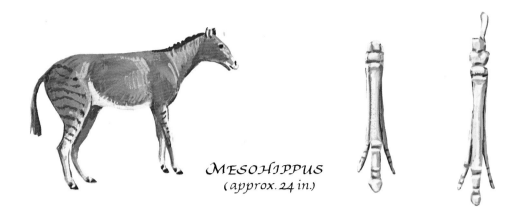

MESOHIPPUS
(approx. 24 in.)

MESOHIPPUS, the first to resemble a small horse, was better equipped for fast running. In MIOHIPPUS the ankle joint became broader and stronger as he adapted to more open grassy country. The placement of the eye socket was changing.

Miocene - Approx. 25 to 10 million years B.C.

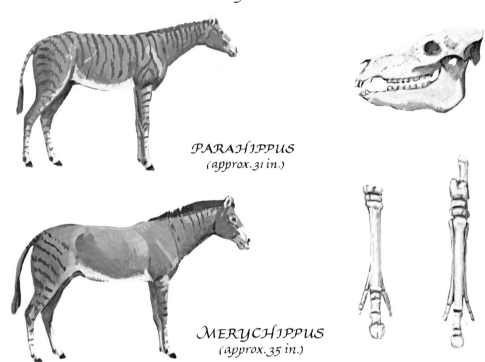

PARAHIPPUS
(approx. 31 in.)

MERYCHIPPUS
(approx. 35 in.)

The most important change noted in PARAHIPPUS was in the grinding ability of the teeth. This indicated a more complete change in diet from browsing to grazing and by MERYCHIPPUS the teeth became more like those of the present day horse.

Pliocene - Approx. 10 to 1 million years B.C.

HIPPARION
(approx. 39 in.)

PLIOHIPPUS
(approx. 44 in.)

HIPPARION crossed from the New to the Old World by the then dry land route through Alaska and Siberia. He flourished throughout Asia and Europe. PLIOHIPPUS was the first one-toed horse in evolutionary history.

Pleistocene - Approx. 1 million to 8,150 years B.C.

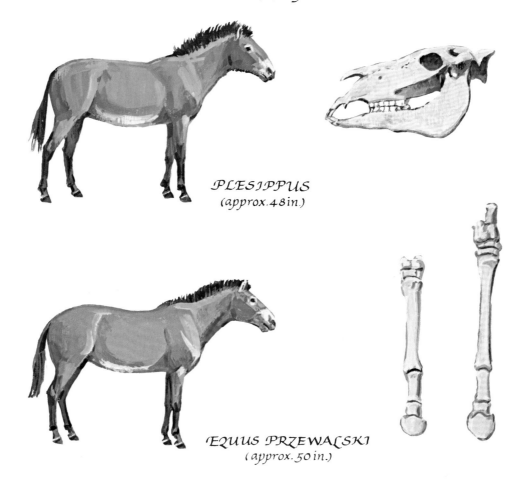

PLESIPPUS
(approx. 48 in.)

EQUUS PRZEWALSKI
(approx. 50 in.)

PLESIPPUS was the final stage of horse evolution. His migration was widespread as fossil remains have been uncovered over most of the world. EQUUS PRZEWALSKI, named after a Russian explorer, was the last wild horse species before man began to establish domestic varieties.

RELATIVES

The NUBIAN ass has a distinct shoulder stripe but no dark markings on the legs. The SOMALI ass has no shoulder or dorsal stripe but has fully striped legs. They are about 12 hands high. Both are African.

BURCHELL'S zebra is the most numerous and best known of all the species. Stocky and about 13 hands he is of the same family as the Chapman's variety. He lives in large herds and prefers the open plains country.

The QUAGGA was a large, chestnut colored, heavily built animal with only the forequarters striped. He abounded throughout South America, but became extinct by 1870. Even skins and photos are rare now.

GREVY's zebra is the largest of the zebra family. The striping is closer and narrower than in other species. It differs from all other zebras in its striding trot (others canter) and with its loud grunt as opposed to a roaring bark.

The modern TARPAN stands between 12 and 13 hands in height. He has a large head with strong massive jaws, a short back and hooves believed to be the toughest in any breed. There is a dorsal stripe and a two-toned mane.

The GRANT's zebra's stripes are broad and on his pasterns they fuse into a continuous black band. In the CHAPMAN's zebra there are faint, narrow stripes between the dark ones. The stripes on the lower legs break up into spots. Both are African.

The KIANG, 13 hands, is larger than the Onager. His body and upper parts are of a reddish tinge, while the ONAGER is generally grayish with sharply defined white areas. Unlike the Kiang he is shy and extremely fast. Both inhabit wild parts of Asia.

The MOUNTAIN zebra dwells in the mountains of Cape Colony, Africa. He stands 12-12½ hands high. The hair on the middle of his back from rump to withers grows forward instead of backward. The throat has a pronounced dewlap (loose fold of skin hanging from neck).

more land in order to establish a ranch where he could raise racehorses. The history of San Simeon's horses is the history of the ranch itself, and the history of the ranch is in turn the history of California, which seems to pass us like a colorful parade of horses. The Spanish soldier-explorers come first on their spirited Andalusian horses, sabers and spurs jingling, and then the padres on docile donkeys ride from mission to mission, teaching the Indians about God and horses. Next come the horse-drawn wagon trains, supplies brought by the Spanish settlers, and the Spanish carts, *carrettas*, rumble by accompanied by *caballeros* on their silver-encrusted saddles.

General Fremont gallops on the scene carrying the American flag and then stagecoaches full of passengers and the United States mail, traveling between San Simeon, San Luis Obispo, San Francisco, and Los Angeles. Ranchers on horses survey their cattle herds, and George Hearst, the newly rich miner, watches his Thoroughbreds race on the track he has built. His wife, Phoebe, in her stylish carriage drawn by high-stepping trotters, is driven from San Luis Obispo to the ranch. Next, their son, young William Randolph, comes riding along with his family and friends to pleasant picnics and campsites in the hills. Heavy-wheeled wagons pulled by draft horses carry stone and lumber up those hills to the campsites where W. R. Hearst starts building his dream castle.

The cavalcade of San Simeon horses features many breeds of horses in many sizes and shapes and colors: Spanish Andalusian horses, Palominos, Thoroughbreds, Morgans, Appaloosas, and finally Quarter Horses, Arabians, Morabs, Welsh ponies, and even Sicilian donkeys and zebras.

Let us look first at the zebras, for surprisingly these relatives of the domestic horse have had a great deal to do with the very existence of this book.

It may seem odd that I wish to begin this book about the horses of San Simeon with an animal that is not even a horse at all but a wild cousin native to the grasslands of Africa. As a child, I knew that proper alphabet books always started with *A* instead of *Z*, and that the *Z* was almost always illustrated with a zebra. But I have two good reasons to reverse that tradition here. First of all, it was a painting by the California artist Bob Reynolds of zebras on the golden hills of San Simeon that planted in me the seed of imagination that eventually resulted in this book. The second reason is perhaps more convincing. Although the domesticated horse *Equus caballus* was first brought to the North Ameri-

can continent by the Spanish explorers, scientists now believe that the first horses developed here millions of years ago, later evolving into zebralike creatures, the ancestors of both the modern horse and the wild zebra. These ancient horses later crossed the land bridge over the Bering Straits from Alaska into Asia, eventually reaching Africa but becoming extinct in the place of their origin. In due course, one genus, *Equus*, would survive, to include all living species of equines. Although the onager and the Mongolian wild horses of Central Asia still exist (the latter only in zoos, being extinct in nature), the zebra still roam their native Africa in large numbers, providing scientists with important insights into the natural behavior of all horses.

At San Simeon tourists gasp and whip out their cameras when they see these striped (the stripes are black *on* white) wild horses of Africa grazing with the ranch cattle. In Africa, of course, zebras share the grasses with relatives of the cow. Wildebeest and zebra feed on the same grasses but do not graze at the same stage of growth as they move in their annual migrations. Zebras are the only plains grazers that have lower and upper incisors, which allow them to bite off mature grasses rather than pluck young shoots.

Burchell's or plains zebras (one of several remaining species) are native to the savannah country from the Sudan down to South Africa, and at times they are numerous enough to resemble a sea of zebras stretching for miles. At San Simeon the Burchell's zebras behave as if they still were on the grasslands of Africa: totally wild, they roam free on thousands of acres of native grassland.

The size of large ponies, weighing perhaps 700 pounds and standing 12 to 14 hands high, the zebra stallions, unlike most other mammals, patrol moveable *property* rather than territory. Harems of mares and foals are protected by one stallion, and these families are followed by troops of immature stallions, the bachelors. In the zebra family the senior mare is second to the family father. She leads, while the stallion guards the rear of the herd, vigilantly alert for stragglers and danger.

At San Simeon, as in Africa, the zebra herd at night beds down while one mare remains on her feet as a lookout. By sunrise, their day begins with a single-file trek, alongside the cows, for a drink of water at a trough or a stream. On rainy, foggy, chilly days they rise later in the morning.

Like horses, zebras enjoy rolling in dust, rubbing themselves on rocks, and grooming each other. Mares groom their foals and stallions groom certain mares, some being preferred over others. The foals of domestic horses respond immediately to being groomed, because social grooming seems to be a deep-seated equine trait. Perhaps it was through grooming that man first tamed and domesticated the wild horse. After grooming, zebras will stand exactly as our domestic horses do, resting their heads on each other's backs for companionship and

Zebra Mare and Foal by Robert Reynolds. This painting of zebras at San Simeon was what originally inspired me to write this book.

safety, since this position gives them a 360-degree view of approaching potential enemies. In California it would not be African lions but mountain lions or coyotes.

Zebras blow with loose lips while grazing, making a sound of contentment much as horses do, but their cry, half a bark and half a bray, sounds nothing like a horse's. When zebra stallions fight, they bite each other but they seldom rear up and paw with their forefeet the way horses do. Zebras can, however, deliver bone-splitting kicks with their hind feet when threatened by predators. Like a horse a zebra stallion will sniff a mare's urine, raise his head, open his mouth, curl back his lip, and test the smell using a special scent organ in order to determine the onset of estrus. This gesture is called "flehmen." At about three years of age females give birth after a gestation period of eleven months to a year. Like other equines mares come into heat a week or so after foaling and every three weeks or so after that until they are pregnant again.

Because the domestic horse and the different species of zebra have different chromosome counts (the horse has sixty-four and the Burchell's zebra only forty-four), they cannot produce fertile young, but these closely related animals can interbreed and their offspring are known as infertile hybrids. The young of a male donkey and a female horse, for example, is a mule, which cannot reproduce itself; the result of a zebra-horse cross is called a zebroid. I have seen some of these in Kenya; they have the faint stripes of their zebra sires and the conformation of their horse dams. Like mules, these hybrids can make strong, surefooted pack animals.

To me, zebras are the handsomest creatures on earth, living works of art. Some experts say the word *zebra* is of Amharic origin meaning "striped," while others claim the word comes from the Hebrew word *tzebi* meaning "beauty or splendor." Evidently William Randolph Hearst thought they were splendid because he imported to his ranch quite a number of Burchell's zebras. Over the years he built up one of the world's largest private collection of various animals. Almost any animal you can think of, from tapirs to elephants, he imported to San Simeon. Because of meat rationing during World War II all the carnivorous animals were given to various zoos, and at the time of his death in 1950, most of the animals that had roamed free were rounded up and sold. An animal dealer wanted the zebras. Before he arrived, in a heavy rainstorm, my husband and I sneaked down to the pens where the zebras had been caged in preparation for shipment and where some of the foals were up to their bellies in mud. We opened the gates and set them all free. As I remember, there must have been about twenty. Many of those remaining today are descendants of that original herd we released.

Like Hearst's guests in the past, tourists today who come to see the castle he built enjoy photographing the zebras. The zebras have been an attraction since the first busload of tourists on their way up to

The horse family (Equidae) has the most complete fossil record of any mammal group, and the earliest known equid is the eohippus, or dawn horse, a four-toed animal slightly larger than a terrier dog which flourished in North America and Europe about fifty million years ago.

see the castle caught sight of them from the window of the bus. In 1958 the State of California, specifically the Department of Beaches and Parks, was given the castle, all its contents, and one-hundred acres of gardens. The rest of the seventy-nine thousand acres still belongs to the Hearst Corporation which gave the state permission to cross their lands and use the road in order to reach the castle. The Hearst Corporation also owns the zebras.

When the herd was diminishing in the 1960s, probably because of age and inbreeding, the state of California persuaded the Hearst Corporation to negotiate with a Los Angeles animal dealer to bring in several young zebra stallions in the hope that they would father some foals. They did the job, and the new foals were born but the stallions have led their bands away from the tourist buses to other parts of the ranch. They do not seem to understand or care how photogenic and exotic they are. Today, two or three widely separated bands range over the ranch, and occasionally they appear near the roads among the cattle where they can be glimpsed from time to time, one of the many different types of equines who have grazed on San Simeon's rich grasses.

Part I/San Simeon–Spanish, Mexican, And American

Chapter 1/The Spanish Explorers

*I will command your fleet and
discover for you new realms.*

—Christopher Columbus

*I*n about 1510 a Spanish explorer named Garcia Ordeonez de
Montalvo wrote in a book entitled *Las Sergas de Esplandian*
"that on the right hand of the Indies there is an island called California."
Thereafter on early maps California was listed as an island. Not until
1542, half a century after Columbus misnamed his discovery in the
Caribbean "the Indies," did another explorer sail up the coast of California. The King of Spain had hired a Portuguese navigator, Juan Rodriguez Cabrillo, to find good harbors for Spanish ships and to look for the
"Strait of Anian" which early cartographers and explorers believed connected the Atlantic and Pacific Oceans somewhere north of Mexico.

Cabrillo's two little ships sailed first into San Diego Bay and
then, following the coast and charting good harbors, he entered San
Simeon Bay. He also mentioned the *Piedras Blancas* ("white rocks") a
name that remains attached to part of the Hearst ranch. He discovered
and described the bay at Monterey, which he named "the Bay of Pines"
for the forests covering the hills.

Farther north, because of heavy fog, Cabrillo entirely missed
the great bay of San Francisco, and, of course, he couldn't find the imag-
inary Strait of Anian. But he had added the whole vast region of
California to Spain's New-World holdings and he was the first European
to see the land that would become San Simeon ranch.

For two centuries Spain did nothing to colonize or develop her
claim. On their way from trading posts in the Philippines to Acapulco in
Mexico and back, the Spanish galleons would sail across the Pacific and
down the coast of California. Although they became familiar with the
Bay of San Simeon and other harbors like it, they seemed to have forgotten their lands in California until England, France, and Russia, all active
in the Pacific, threatened to snatch them away in the middle of the
eighteenth century.

In 1602 an explorer named Sebastian Vizcaino had landed at
the Bay of Pines and renamed it after the Count of Monterey. He had

The *Piedras Blancas,* or
white rocks, were named
by a Spanish explorer in
the sixteenth century,
and the cattle ranch on
the Hearst land still bears
the name today.

3

NUEVO

MEXICO

Apaches
o'
DE NAVAIO

Apaches de

XILA.   Taofii.

Agubela de Cato

R. de Estrete

Mar

Talaago

C. Blanco
C. de S.
Sebastian

C. de Mendocino

Pte de los Reyes

Pte de Monte Rey

Pto de Francisco Draco

Pte de Carinda

P. de la Conception

Canal de S. Barbara

B. de la Conversion

P. de S. Diego

I. S. Cathalina

S. Clement.

I. S. Martin

I. de Parraros

I. S. Marco

I. de Ceintas

I. de la Carre

Pta
de Roqui

Mer

De

Sud   ou

Ligne fous le Tropicque du Cancer.

Punta de S.
Apollinat.

B. de S.
Martin

Pto de la
Magdalena

P. de la Marque

P. de Cenou

P. de la Paz

B. Bernabe

C. de S. Lucas

PACIFICQUE.

Californie Isle

Rey Coromedo

Lago
de
Oro

R. de Aquche

R. de Tizon

R. de Coral

I. de Gigante

las Playas

S. Miguel

Pto de S.
Clara

Mar

Vermeio.

R. de S.
Christoval

B. de S.
Francisco

B. de S. Simon

P. de S. Bartolomeo

Sierra Pintado

B. de las
Arenas

B. de las
Virgines

C. de
Engaño

B. de S. Quintu

B. de Todos los
Santos

Zaguato

Zuni als

Cibola.

Moqui.

GRA

Apaches
DE
PERILLO.

NUE VA

Acoma

Ameies.

Cumaues
STA FE.

Queres.

Tebes

Souilletta
Pilabo

Piri
Seneu
Socorro

Cia.

Tami.

Tigues.

Hubates.

Nueva Mexico.

Peici

Tompires.

Gorretes.

Manfes.

NA

VA

MARATA REGNVM.

R. del Norte

Hanes.

Sumes.

Tomites.

Tepoanes.

Tarrahumares.

S. Francisco
Petarlan
C.

Astetlan.

Ometlan.

CINALOA.

DA.

Iumanes.

Tobofes.

Paffaguates.

Conches.

Nue va

Bis

Endehe

Culiacan

S. Michael

Quinaloa.

Cain

Durango
M. de Avino

Nombre
de Dios

Mar
tin

Ellerena

Xeres

Guadalaiara
Compostella

Las Tres
Marias

Las Tres
Marias

N

Early mapmakers thought that California was an island, as shown on this French map made by Nicolas Sanson in 1656.

275 280 285 290 295 300 305

50

ADA

LE NOUVEAU MEXIQUE,
et LA FLORIDE :
Tirées de diverses Cartes, et Relations.
Par N. Sanson d'Abbeville Geogr ord.re du Roy.
A PARIS.
Chez Pierre Mariette, Rue S. Iacque a l'Esperance.
Avec Privilege du Roy, pour vingt Ans.
1656.

OUVEL=

Mont Real 45

Sault de S.
Louys.
R. S. Laurens.
I. Capaqui
chissins

Akiatoenonon.

ONTARIO, ou
LAC DE S. LOUIS.

Assistaero
nous ou
N. du Feu.

Couacronon

L. des Eaux
de Mer

Ongiara
Sault

Sovoua
renou

Aictaeronon.

S. Ioseph

ERIE LAC

Eriech
ronons

VIRGI=

LE FRANCE

Capachi Calicuas

Squenquio
ronon

Oatarra=
ronon.

NIE.

Naguater

Chiasca Canasraguay Xuala

Chalaque

Attiouan=
darous

Tali

Vlibahali Guazula

Aminoja

Cofachiqui

Nisoona

Cosle

DE

Anileo

Guancane

Apalatchi

Montes

FLORIDE

Chagus

Yehiaba

Cofagui

Cofa

Apalache

COISE.

Lacane

Coza Acoste

Grsacacoya

Naguatex

Achalaque

Matiqua

Anatequa
Edelano

Staslane

Caroline

Chillano

Capaha

Vtianuque

Ossachile

Hustaqua

Vtina

Timaco

FRAN=

Ayx

Ouiga ta

Chasquin

Tula

Colima

Vitacucho

Ocile

Saturiva

Xualatino

Chisca

Quigu ate

S. Iulius

Ocali

Virri Bara

Sarope

Achusi

Tascalasa

Ancon Baxo

Guax

Mucosso

S. Petro

B. de Tate
baga

S. Matheo

S. Augustin

B. de S.
Ioseph

Barra de
S. Matheo

B. de Matruças

MER

Herrihigua

LE.

B. de Tegesta

Baira de Mosquitos

R. das Pescadores

C. Baxo
R. Suelo

Plaia

C. de Suerta

R. Lago

B. de
Tampa

C. Carlos

B. de
Carlos

Abra de
Canaveral

C. de Canaveral

Escuda de Aix

TERLICHI=
CHIME=
CHI.

Galos

Escondido

Costa
Deserta
R.

R. de la Magdalena

C. Blanco

R. de Oro

R. Bravo

R. de los Al
garefos

C. Espiritu

Punta
de S.
Iulia

Provin
DE

Culias

R. Solo

la Punta Bua

B. de Iuan
Ponce

Vachus

R. de Palmas

R. Bravo

Costa de Pescadores

GOLFO DE

C. d'Aguada

B. d'Aguada

C. de
Florida

Cabeça de
los Martyres

Canal de Bahama

huneca

Turmeo

Salinas

S. Bartolome

R. Ermoso

los
Martyres

Roques

25

PA NU

Ligne sous le Tropicque du Cancer.

NORT.

S. Iago de las
Valles

PANUCO

R. Panuco

Taxithan

PANUCO

C. Roxo

LA HAVANA

Sta Cruz

 Michel

CO.

Lobos I.

CUBA ISLE.

AGNE.

MEXICOUE.

C S. Antonio

C. Corientes

270 MEXICO 275 280 285 290 Somer Sculp. 295

This map of the "island" of California was made by an Englishman, John Speed, in 1676.

CVSCO · MOCA in Chili · RIAN EIRO · OLINDA

PART OF SPAINE EUROPA

PART OF AFRICA

Streight of Davis

Hudfons Straight

NEWE BRITTAINE

ERNE

Canada

Newe England

THE ATLANTICKE

Frisland

Part of Groenland

I. das Demonies

Afores or

Wefterne Ilands

The Fortunate

or Canaries Ilands

THE

OCEAN

The Bermudas now called the Sommer Ilands

The Tropicke of Cancer

NORTH

Hifpanniola

S. Antonio

Ý I. of C. Verde

C. Verde

SEA

GUIANA

Amazones

Iwaipanoma

THE

BRASI LIA

SOUTHERNE PART

Tabaiar

GUAIRA

Toupinikini Morpion Carion

CUMANIA

OF AMERICA

Rio de la Plata that is the silver river

Patagones

CHICA

The Streight of le Maire was firft found the year 1616 by Iacob le Maire

Abraham Goos Amftelodamenfis fculpfit

PERUVIANE

BRASILIANE

BRASILIANE fculp

A MOCHAN

MAGELLANICAN

39

recommended that Spain start a colony there. Not until 1769, however, did the King of Spain, Carlos III, decide to establish two colonies, one at Monterey and one at San Diego. He ordered José de Galvez, the governor of New Spain (Mexico), to explore and colonize Alta (upper) California.

Four expeditions left Mexico, two ships and two land companies, and they planned to meet in San Diego, but only a sorry lot—ill, starving, and disheartened—managed to reach the rendezvous. One ship, half-manned by now, was sent back to Mexico for supplies and one land group comprising sixty-four men who could still stand up, started north, led by Captain Gaspar de Portola. They wisely carried provisions and water in flasks and casks, and they even included feed for their horses. In San Diego they left behind a Franciscan priest and dedicated missionary named Father Junipero Serra who had been chosen by the King of Spain to head the religious part of the expedition and to convey the Catholic faith to the Indians. He was to found the first mission and await the return of the supply ship.

The land group, hacking through the wilderness too far inland, missed the harbor at Monterey for which they were looking, but farther north they did discover San Francisco Bay. Realizing they had come too far, they struggled back to San Diego. The supply ship had finally returned and the others they had left behind greeted them joyfully. Once again the priests and soldiers headed north, back toward Monterey. Six weeks later they found the bay and claimed the land for Spain. On the way, they had walked along the beaches and camped in two locations on what was to become the Hearst ranch at San Simeon.

Father Serra had founded his first mission and church at San Diego and now at Monterey he planned his second. As he celebrated his first mass there, the Spanish royal flag waved overhead and the statue of the Blessed Virgin that he had carried on the long arduous trip from Mexico was put on a makeshift altar. In 1771, Father Serra founded his third mission, San Antonio de Padua, over the hills in the nearby river valley. He was determined to annex the land along the ocean as part of his mission property. It was named Rancho de la Piedra Blanca for the big rocks offshore, whitened by thousands of sea birds perching there over the years. The white rocks could even be seen by passing ships many miles at sea.

Steadfast and indomitable, Father Serra went on founding his missions, one after the other. Only with great difficulty could they be supplied with food, horses, cows, and other domestic animals and farm equipment. All had to come by boat or over the mountains and deserts. Four hundred miles of wild country lay between Monterey and San Diego and still more between San Diego and Mexico City. Little by little, however, after the third mission, San Antonio de Padua, was established inland from San Simeon, Father Serra's missions began to be

Pico Creek

self-sufficient, even to prosper. In addition to the Christian faith the Indians were taught trades by the Spanish craftsmen imported by the mission fathers. They learned masonry, carpentry, weaving, tailoring, farming, and animal husbandry—in short, the Spanish way of life.

Conversion was voluntary but, once baptized, Indians were required to live at the mission where they were fed, housed, and clothed. Mission records kept lists of baptisms, showing that whole villages of Indians were put to work under Spanish overseers, constructing the mission buildings, raising the animals and the food, grinding the grain, and baking the bread. The California coastal Indians had been primarily dependent on hunting, fishing, and food gathering before the Spanish came. They had many different dialects, beliefs, and rituals which the Spanish priests did not understand or simply chose to ignore. They felt that such practices had to be stamped out and they punished Indians who did not want to give up their old ways and ceremonies honoring the sun and the seasons. The Indians must have felt they were in prison, being forced to work for the Spanish and to pray in churches away from their seashores, meadows, and forests. Occasionally they tried to fight, to escape, but their resistance was always fiercely and bloodily suppressed.

Thus began the mission story. It lasted sixty-four years and in the end the whole imperialistic effort seemed to have been futile, but it stamped California forever with the imprint of Spain.

In California around San Simeon the climate reminded the Spanish of their homeland: game was abundant, and plants flourished in this remarkably fertile land. Of course neither the Indians nor the Spanish knew that about 180 million years earlier the whole area had been under the Pacific Ocean. Volcanic action that took place about 20 million years ago created the great rocks which can be seen in what is now San Luis Obispo County. Volcanic cores were also eroded under the ocean. Still later, geological uplift formed the Santa Lucia Mountains, which extend the length of that part of the coast. The only thorn on this rosy terrain is the earthquake belt, for the San Andreas Fault runs right through the area.

Piedra Blanca |

Chapter 2/The Missions and Ranches

Hast thou given the horse strength?
Hast thou clothed his neck with thunder?
He paweth in the valley and rejoiceth
in his strength; he goeth on to meet
the armed men. He mocketh at fear
and is not affrighted; neither turneth
he back from the sword.

—The Book of Job

*T*he bay of San Simeon was named by a devout early Spanish settler to honor an old man in the New Testament who was one of the first to hail Jesus as the long-awaited Messiah. According to the book of Saint Luke, Simeon had been promised by God that he would not die until he had seen the Saviour:

> *Now there was a man in Jerusalem whose name was Simeon ...*
> *and the Holy Spirit was upon him ... and inspired by the Holy*
> *Spirit he came into the temple and when the parents brought in the*
> *child Jesus to do for him according to the custom of the law, he took*
> *him in his arms and blessed God and said, "Lord, now let thy*
> *servant depart in peace, according to thy word. For mine eyes have*
> *seen thy salvation...."*

Whether the soldiers, the sailors, or the friars who gave the name had a particular devotion to the saint or simply arrived at the bay on the saint's feast day, we do not know.

When the mission San Miguel Arcángel was established, by Father Lasuen, in 1797, after the death of Father Serra in 1784, the mission claimed the land west all the way over to the ocean, below the bay of San Simeon. The nearest mission neighbor to the north, San Antonio de Padua, owned the northern portion of the land on the coast. These two former mission holdings are today the southern and northern parts of the Hearst ranch.

At San Miguel the priests hoped that water would be plentiful for farming. Unlike neighboring San Antonio de Padua, the San Miguel mission saw the Salinas River go dry and disappear underground for months at a time. Nevertheless, nearby springs were abundant and an

Mission Cattle Drive by Sam Savitt. California Indians, converted by the Franciscan missionaries, learned to tend the mission herds of longhorned cattle and to ride their horses of Spanish Andalusian breeding. This painting shows the Indians driving cattle from their mountain pastures down to the bay of San Simeon.

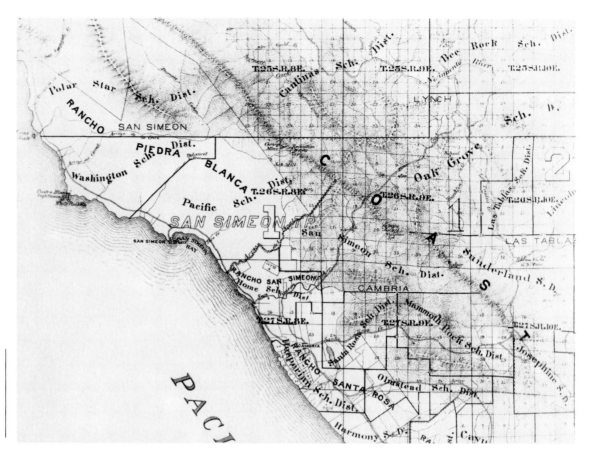

This detail of a map of San Luis Obispo County, published in 1899, shows the three ranches—Piedra Blanca, San Simeon, and Santa Rosa.

irrigation system constructed by the mission to harness the spring water can still be traced. On the coastal land where streams flowed and rain fell more abundantly, farming was easier.

In early mission records this portion of their property was known as "the ocean ranch." In 1810, only thirteen years after founding the mission, the priests set up an outpost and began trading with the passing ships. The harbor at San Simeon Bay offered an ideal protected anchorage, deep water, and a sandy, sloping beach for landing. Ships could replenish their fresh vegetables and fruit, take on hides and, above all, fine horses, for the horses raised by the mission priests were much in demand. The sea captains could sell them profitably in other ports even as far away as Hawaii. All the missions' horses and cows were marked with brands as was customary in Spain. San Miguel's registered brand was a flat-topped number three which represented the Holy Trinity.

Extensive research about San Miguel and San Antonio was published in 1920 by a mission historian, Father Zephyrin Engelhardt. He believed that buildings and corrals for holding horses were constructed at San Simeon ranch as early as 1810. In spite of a crippling fire in 1806 which had destroyed the San Miguel mission buildings, six thousand bushels of wheat, and a great deal of wool and hides, the mission was rebuilt and an outpost finished at San Simeon by 1810. Broodmares, pastured at liberty on the hills, were the mission's most numerous domestic animals and their offspring were eagerly sought by the passing traders. Sizeable profits in gold, furs, and other valuable items were amassed by the mission fathers; indeed, the pious priests were surprisingly vulpine. They lived comfortably but were rather quiet about sending reports back to Mexico accounting for their activities. They never even referred to the San Simeon ranch until 1827, and they downplayed their wealth and the numbers of their animals. Certainly their most valuable possessions were the coastal ranches, rich with fertile soil, ample water from springs and streams, woodlands, rolling pastures and, of course, the bounty from the sea.

Each day the diet of the residents at the inland missions was supplemented by seafood brought across the hills by Indian runners using the age-old trails. Quail and other game hunted on their coastal domains also provided the missions with feasts. Years earlier in 1771 members of the second Portola expedition searching along the coast to find the harbor of Monterey had stopped when they reached the northern part of what is now the Hearst ranch where impassable mountains come right down to the sea. The explorers were forced to turn inland where they followed some of the Indian paths that wandered through the mountain passes from the coast to the valleys beyond. These Indian footpaths had run up the coast for countless centuries before the Spanish used them. A member of that expedition, Father Juan Crespi, wrote in his journal that "we descended to the shore and followed it along good trails, northwesterly along the cliffs." Several journals kept by members of the party mentioned the good trails and the generous, gentle Indians. They told about camping and exploring the mountains along the Indians' well-worn footpaths.

The bureaucratic problems of administering colonies from the other side of the ocean finally toppled the royal rule of Spain. In 1821, not too many years after the neighboring United States had won freedom from England, Mexico broke away from Spain and in 1822 California became a province of the new republic of Mexico. A governor was sent to take up residence in Monterey.

After many years of expanding their herds, their crops, and their buildings, the missions were rich, powerful, and remote. Meanwhile, the smell of revolt against the church drifted slowly up to Monterey and Santa Barbara. The old establishment still revered the clergy, if not the crown of Spain, but the passionate younger men argued and won autonomy for parts of the republic of Mexico and agitated against the domination of the church. Increasing Yankee immigration also spread ideas of freedom. In spite of much discord between northern and southern California (for example, Monterey and Los Angeles each claimed to be the true capital), they did completely agree on one point: if they could pry loose the land and holdings of the church, huge wealth would be available for distribution. The twenty-one missions controlled eight million acres of prime land, more than 150,000 head of horses, cattle, and sheep, as well as profitable trade with many foreign ships and a labor pool of thousands of Indian workers.

And so, in 1824, the Secularization Act was authorized by the Mexican Constitution. Ten years of tumult and foot-dragging followed, until finally the missions were forced to give up their land and livestock. The priests were ordered to turn over their buildings to the Mexican government. The Indians were told to leave their houses around the missions. During the governorship of Alvarado half the missions' horses were sold, two-thirds of the cattle and three-fourths of the sheep were slaughtered. The friars and their Indian wards did not receive the pay they had been promised, and the land to be distributed to the Indians somehow evaporated. The Indians were tragic figures in many cases. They had spent their lives under the strict authority of the missions and had lost their ancient ways of life. Their numbers had seriously decreased, from fifteen thousand to less than five thousand by 1829. When offered freedom, they were confused, uncertain of the world outside. Some of them drifted into the nearest towns and villages where they were further demoralized by liquor, disease, and exploitation. The more fortunate ones went to work for the new ranch owners.

A Franciscan and his Mount by Sam Savitt

Father Junipero Serra by Sam Harris. This portrait of the Franciscan missionary shows the many missions he founded along the California coast.

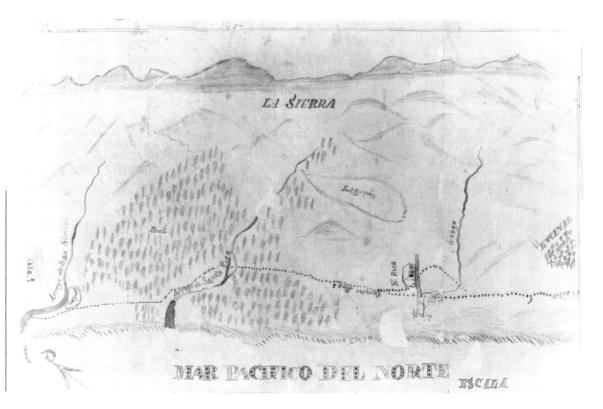

In 1842 Julian Estrada obtained from the Mexican government a grant for the Rancho Santa Rosa. After California was ceded to the United States in 1848, Estrada filed a claim, supported by this map, in order to have his grant validated under United States law. In 1876 Santa Rosa was sold to George Hearst.

By 1834 the mission buildings of San Miguel were already falling into ruins as were those of San Antonio de Padua. The priests were gone, but the mission lands had not been distributed either to homesteaders or to the few remaining Indians. Only a few Spanish land grants had been made before 1821 because Spain's colonial policy had centered on building the missions and military forts or *presidios.* One of the few grants was made by the Spanish governor, Pedro Fages, in 1784 as a result of his decision to hand out large tracts of land to his comrades-at-arms and cronies. One Juan José Dominguez, for example, in recognition for his services as guide, soldier, and Indian interpreter, received a grant of seventy-five thousand acres. Today, millions of Californians live on that same land, which is now part of Los Angeles, Redondo Beach, and other towns. The adobe residence of the Rancho San Pedro still stands, a national historical landmark. This land is the only Spanish grant of which a section is still owned by descendants of the original grantees.

After secularization in the new country of Mexico, a person with friends in the government usually got special consideration. So the choice pieces of land were grabbed by the same Mexican government administrators appointed to supervise the cutting of the missions' fat pie of lands.

Don José Jesus de Pico was sent to administer the distribution of lands belonging to the San Antonio mission, and he later became administrator for San Miguel mission lands. At first, however, his friend José Mariano Estrada was in charge of San Miguel, and in 1842 Estrada obtained the Rancho San Simeon for one son, José Ramon, and the Rancho Santa Rosa for another son. Young José Ramon Estrada did not have to fulfill the three standard requirements for obtaining a grant —namely to build a house, fill the land with livestock, and plant an orchard—because all of these already existed at Rancho San Simeon.

At the San Antonio mission, the Mexican administrator Don Pico managed to get the mission's best lands for himself. He had appealed to Governor Alvarado for a grant of the Rancho Piedra Blanca and he received it in 1840. His prize was gigantic; all the land up to the top of the mountains and south of San Carpoforo (now shortened to San Carpojo Creek) constituted about 136 square miles, or almost forty-nine thousand acres.

Don Pico continued to have many connections with the changing, turbulent government in Monterey for he was a cousin of Pio Pico who became governor after Alvarado, having helped Mexico in her

Mission San Miguel Arcángel by H. M. T. Powell. This pencil drawing, made on April 4, 1850, shows the extensive outbuildings used for housing Indian converts and sheltering livestock.

San Miguel.

fight to win freedom from Spain. Some years later, Don Pico persuaded a foreign visitor, the French cartographer Eugène Dufolt de Mofras, to study and map his new ranch, Piedra Blanca. The young Frenchman did so, and he also produced the first good map of the whole Pacific coast. He wrote an accompanying volume which noted that the bay at San Simeon was regularly used "as an excellent harbor."

Don Pico, as the new owner of the Piedra Blanca Ranch, in order to comply with land-grant laws of Mexico, built a house for his family, brought in more Spanish longhorn cattle, and employed Indians to tend his herd. His adobe home, occupied only occasionally, overlooked a creek not far from the ocean, south of San Simeon Bay. Today, the stables for our Arabian horses face the same meandering stream which is called Pico's Creek.

Many Mexican dons enjoyed riding around in Spanish sombreros, trimmed like their saddles in silver and gold, and they used any excuse for a *fiesta*—a marriage, a cattle branding, a Holy Day. For these *fiestas*, distant friends, family, and neighbors would arrive on horseback or in *carretas*, rough two-wheeled carts often drawn by oxen instead of horses. They would dance, sing, drink, feast, and watch bullfights and displays of horsemanship.

Even with frequent fiestas, the Pico family found life on this remote property dull, isolated, and too distant from the politics and people they enjoyed, and so they visited the ranch perhaps twice a year. In actual fact, the coastal ranches at Piedra Blanca, San Simeon, and Santa Rosa were hardly occupied at all by their owners, the Picos and Estradas, although one Estrada son, Julian, did eventually move with his wife and family to Rancho Santa Rosa.

The Pico family of Piedra Blanca and the Estradas of San Simeon and Santa Rosa had to fend off many land thieves who wished to take away their land. For example, in 1842 a certain José Miguel Gomez had been sent to oversee affairs at the San Miguel mission. He found that the mission's coastal land had already been spoken for by the Estradas, but he nevertheless applied for a grant in his own name. The coastal ranch of San Simeon was what Gomez wanted, but he lost out when Governor Alvarado awarded it to his friend Estrada applying on behalf of his son.

When José Ramon Estrada became ill and died suddenly, his death brought about the sale of his San Simeon property to a man named Thomas Park, who sold it in turn to a Henry Pefft. Finally, the same José Miguel Gomez who had lost out in the beginning stepped in, paid $2000 cash plus a note for $500, and moved into the building that was the Rancho San Simeon.

But the land would not long remain in Mexican hands, for the Americans were waiting in the wings to push the Mexicans out of the spotlight of history.

Chapter 3/San Simeon Turns American

Oh! Not all the pleasure that poets may praise
Not the wildering waltz in the ball-room's blaze,
Nor the chivalrous joust, nor the daring race,
Nor the swift regatta, nor merry chase,
Nor the sail high heaving waters o'er,
Nor the rural dance on the moonlight shore,
Can the wild and fearless joy exceed
Of a fearless leap on a fiery steed.

—Sara J. Clarke

*J*ust as the Spanish had taken over the lands of the Indians, just as the Mexican settlers had forced the missions to give up their lands, so the Mexicans were in turn to lose much of their land and their political power in California.

The Californians were generous, graceful, and pleasure loving. They welcomed the first American settlers who came overland and swore allegiance to Mexico, married local women, and joined in the rounds of religious holidays, dancing, guitar playing and horse racing.

An immense, sparsely peopled province, always an outpost, California was considered a godforsaken end of the earth by Mexicans in the seat of government at Mexico City. The government offered land and other inducements and finally had to empty the jails to lure colonists to California. Many of these new colonists were convicts and low-caste Mexicans, pathetic and half-starved ruffians, more fit for brawling, thieving, drinking, and trouble making than for colonizing California. The few established settlers scorned the new arrivals, referred to them as *cholos* ("scoundrels"). It was these same *cholos* who would team up with the American settlers on the frontiers to hatch a rebellion.

The new colonists called themselves "Californios" rather than Mexicans and their loyalty was focused on their own localities, such as Monterey, Santa Barbara, or Los Angeles, rather than on the faraway government in Mexico City. In addition, the government was too shaky, too preoccupied with political fights to care about happenings in barbarous California.

Mexican Don Coming to Town by Sam Savitt

Down on the Texas border, American settlers had proclaimed themselves a "republic" free of Mexican rule and, in similar fashion, the

55

My brave associates, partners of my toil, my feelings, and my
which inspire your hearts no! you have judg'd as I
would delude, you, they seek time only for the villain
note of preparation for scenes of deeper carnage is st
wave their ensanguined folds o'r the chains of th
now, ah ———— a — e e — horrid sight — boy g
forward and storm the works there is only
Music strike up ——

Taking of Monterey Oct 20th 1842 by the
frigate United States & Sloop of War Cyane — Lat 36° 3

The Taking of Monterey by William Meyers. This painting was made by an American sailor who saw and recorded the event on

Americans and a few *cholos* plotted a Texas-type coup in California. Since there was no Mexican army to fight, a Mexican general would do. Therefore, on an early June morning in 1846, a group of Americans marched into the rancho home of general Mariano Vallejo in northern California at Sonoma. They declared they were forming a "Yankee Republic" and took the general captive. While they were drafting their articles of capitulation, Vallejo, an affable admirer of Americans, offered them a bottle of wine. They took the wine and also took his brother Salvador and his American son-in-law Jacob Leese and transported them all to Fort Sutter where Captain John Charles Fremont was in command of a small American force. Fremont had been stationed there by the United States government, ostensibly to map and explore the country and to protect American citizens in the area. President Polk and the United States government were playing a cautious diplomatic game. They did indeed covet California but wished to annex it, if possible, without provoking war with Mexico. However, the hotheads, not caring whether or not they precipitated a war, proclaimed themselves the independent "Bear Flag Republic." Fremont became their new leader and the "Bear Flaggers" captured and held prisoners such as the unfortunate General Vallejo. They terrorized northern California with shootings, pillage, and confiscation along with desperate talk of liberating California from Mexican oppression.

Even with their General Vallejo ignominiously treated as a prisoner, the Mexican government neglected to act, hoping it would all blow over, as it had done some years before in 1842 when an American commodore, Thomas ap Catesby Jones, sailed his ship, the *United States*, into the harbor of Monterey and captured it without even trying.

Falsely believing that Mexico and the United States were already at war, Commodore Jones sent his demand for the surrender of Monterey by mistake to the former governor of California, Alvarado. Alvarado, although no longer the governor, asked town officials to a meeting at his hacienda to discuss the situation. Everyone agreed that twenty-nine soldiers, twenty-five militiamen, and eleven cannons without ammunition could not resist the American ship, and so the town surrendered and the American flag was hoisted over Monterey. Then the next day, the commodore was informed that the United States and Mexico were *not* at war, and he lowered the American flag and ran the Mexican flag back up. He sent an apology, returned Monterey to the Mexicans, and everyone had a joint celebration.

The flag of Mexico waved over California for a few more years. When Fremont and the Bear Flaggers proclaimed their Yankee Republic, they stirred up a fire. Californians feared Fremont and were worried that the United States would take over their province.

Because Fremont had expanded his activities, Commodore John D. Sloat of the United States Pacific Squadron became convinced

PRESIDIO OF MONTERREY

Presidio of Monterey | that Fremont was acting on orders from the United States. Sloat had orders himself from Washington that if war came he was to take the California ports. So he sailed the American ships *Portsmouth, Levant,* and *Cyane* into Monterey harbor. The U. S. ship *Savannah* sailed in next and dropped anchor. For four days Sloat waited peacefully. Then being uncertain and fearing that the Californians might raise an army or the British fleet might arrive, he ignored the advice of the American consul in Monterey, Mr. Larkin, and landed a force of two hundred and fifty marines. The American flag was hoisted over the customs house while the band played and the ships' guns saluted. Monterey was taken.

Sloat promised the Mexican citizens the same rights and privileges as Americans. Thanks to fast horses, the news galloped to other California towns and soon The Stars and Stripes were being hoisted all along the coast. The Bear Flag Republic was declared null and void. The transition, however, from Mexico to the United States, would not take place without some fighting. By 1847 the guns of war blasted away, but the Mexican war would be all over in only sixteen months. As a final brave stand, a group of Mexicans on horseback led by Andrés Pico, the governor's brother, met General Stephen W. Kearny's Americans in one last fight.

BAY OF MONTEREY UPPER CALIFORNIA

Bay of Monterey, Upper California (artist unknown)

But the war ended in absolute victory for the United States under the command of General Winfield Scott, a battle-scarred soldier who some years later led the United States Army against the Confederacy. After the Mexican war, James Russell Lowell wrote that it was "the *manifest destiny* of the English race to occupy this whole continent." Perhaps it was the Americans' easy victory over the Mexicans that emboldened them to dash headlong into the bloodiest war in our history, the Civil War.

For a few years, in theory, the Californios and the Yankees would govern California together. In practice, however, the Mexican leaders, such as the former governor Alvarado, went into retirement. Although many of the younger men participated in the California legislature, the confusion of state politics (the Constitution had both Spanish and English versions) and the clash of different heritages gradually estranged the Mexicans from the political mainstream. Influential and wealthy families like the Picos had lost their country but they still seemed to enjoy life. They could laugh that they had lost some of their best riding horses to the Americans.

The value of the horses was small compared to what Mexico had lost. With the Treaty of Hildalgo, signed in 1848, Mexico gave the

United States all of California, Utah, and what is now Nevada, Arizona, New Mexico, and parts of Colorado and Wyoming. That same year, about 150 miles east of San Francisco, James Wilson Marshall who worked for John A. Sutter, owner of a Mexican grant of land and a mill, saw shining in the sun in Mr. Sutter's millrace some metallic sparkles— gold! Gold was discovered and all hell broke loose.

Gradually, after 1848, the land holdings of the native Mexican-Californians began to diminish. Former Mexican dons had difficulty getting men to work their herds of horses and cows, and they suffered from droughts and absentee ownership. They waged legal battles to prove to the United States the boundary lines of their Mexican grants, and these government surveys and ownership disputes went on until 1859 with much wrangling and many legal discussions. For example, the original grant to the Estrada brothers had stated that the San Simeon and Santa Rosa ranches bordered each other. However, after the American occupation, an official United States survey left a large tract not owned by either ranch. This difference of many acres became available to American homesteaders as public domain.

Even though the Gomez family ranch, San Simeon, shrank after the government survey, it rose in value when it was next sold in 1856, together with Gomez's livestock and his brand, to one Jerome Limas. Limas in turn sold the property to Domingo Pujol in 1857 for the price of $5,000. Don Pujol had married Doña Ramona Cabrillo Pacheco, whose family already owned part of the adjoining Piedra Blanca ranch. Don Pujol and his law firm made loans requiring land as collateral to many of the once-Mexican dons, who needed money and lawyers to prove their ownership according to United States laws. In this way, he soon amassed a huge number of acres, just in time to satisfy the land-hungry Americans who were arriving every month. Don Pujol sold the acres of San Simeon to one Ira Van Gorden, who had been at Sutter's Mill when gold was discovered. The new owner was determined to divide and sell his property as small parcels.

By 1854 Don José Jesus de Pico had sold a large chunk of the Piedra Blanca grant to his close friend, Romualdo Pacheco. This sale included one-half of the acreage around the bay of San Simeon. Proving ownership boundaries according to the new United States government regulations had been costly, and Pico's absentee management had not been efficient. In addition to the sale, he gave various plots to his children. Ten years later, he was bankrupt with debt and his herds of horses and longhorn cattle had been destroyed by drought, hunger, and neglect.

In 1865, a miner named George Hearst bought whatever parts of the Piedra Blanca Ranch Pico would sell, including land below the creek where Pico had his adobe house and the parts around the bay. Hearst planned to sell some of the land around the beach, but since two

Fremont's Ride to the White House (artist unknown). When Major John C. Fremont accepted California's capitulation from Mexican officials in 1847, he gained a great deal of popularity as a political figure. In 1856 he was nominated by the new Republican party as a presidential candidate but was subsequently defeated by James Buchanan.

FREMONT'S RIDE TO THE WHITE HOUSE.

of Don Pico's sons had homes there, Hearst agreed to deed back that acreage to their father. Hearst also added piece by piece to his southern boundary, buying up as fast as Van Gorden and others would sell.

Before the advent of George Hearst, the protected little harbor at San Simeon had become a busy center for hunting whales. Around 1852 they began hunting from the shore, the oldest type of whaling. Whales had long since disappeared from the shores of the east coast, and New England ships from such ports as Nantucket had been forced to follow their quarry around the Horn into the Pacific. Since the gigantic mammals could still be captured along the California coast, small vessels from San Simeon harbor could set out after the gray whales during their annual migration from Alaska to Mexico and return before winter.

One whaler, Joseph Clark, and his crew hunted off San Simeon for thirty years. The whales, both gray and humpback, would be harpooned and towed in dead or dying, until their blood reddened the waters of the little bay. Their carcasses would then be hoisted to shore by a cable-and-pulley system and flensed (stripped of blubber). The large iron pots used to render the oil from the blubber can still be seen in the area. The town of Cambria, near San Simeon, still remembers the whaling days with an annual festival. In the tiny hamlet of San Simeon a state historical landmark, Sebastian's Store, dates back to those whaling days and still sells general merchandise. Moved on rollers in the late nineteenth century from a bluff overlooking the harbor down to the town, the store today sells hundreds of items to tourists as it once did to whalers.

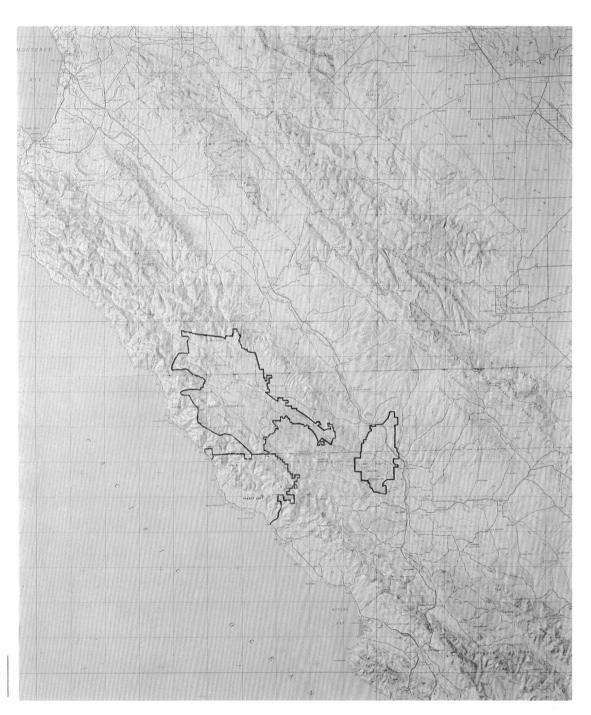

This relief map shows in outline the boundaries of San Simeon Ranch.

The whaling station land and other property around the point of the Piedra Blanca was what Don Pico had sold to Romualdo Pacheco in 1854, and it was inherited by Pacheco's children, Marianna, Juana, Maria Ynacia, Ramona, and John. They made Hearst wait for months and years, discussing and negotiating for pieces of the land. One of the heirs, who had married into the Castro family, leased land along San Carpojo Creek to a group of dairy farmers, who purchased some of this land.

Doggedly, year by year, acre by acre, George Hearst added to his ranch. Always his ready money, earned by brains and sweat in the mining fields, was spent on the land. He had various schemes and hopes that he could generate some income from these growing acquisitions. He obtained permission from the county to build a wharf and pier in partnership with Joseph Lull and Captain Joseph Clark, who owned parcels of land and the whaling station at San Simeon Bay. Hearst proposed selling lots around the pier, for he believed that the nearby dairymen and farmers would ship their produce from there. He would collect fees for their use of the pier and warehouses, and the town would prosper, for it had such a fine harbor. The area was producing many cattle for hides and dairy products as well as horses, timber, and cinnabar. Everything and anything could be shipped from the harbor at San Simeon to markets north and south.

By 1869 a wharf and pier were completed. Calling themselves Grant, Lull and Company, Hearst and his partners put up another warehouse and a store in 1872. By 1878 they had built yet another pier, which extended a thousand feet into deep water and a roadway twenty feet wide, over which narrow-gauge railway tracks were laid. A newer and larger warehouse was constructed.

In the meantime Julian Estrada, who was still owner of the Santa Rosa ranch, struggled to get his original grant approved by the United States and to make his property support itself. He had his longhorn cattle driven over the trails to San Francisco markets, for after the Gold Rush in 1849, meat was more valuable than gold in San Francisco. Mostly, he sold hides, shipped out of various ports along the coast. When a ship landed at one port, a courier would gallop to the next port to announce that the ship was headed their way. Ranchers would then bring their hides by horse-drawn wagons to await the vessel's arrival. San Simeon Bay and Leffingwell Landing, a few miles down the coast, became regular ports of call for Estrada. As more settlers moved in, trails and tracks became wider cart roads. In spite of his hard, loving labor for his land, Julian died disappointed and in debt. His oldest son, Francisco, nicknamed "Pancho," was only seventeen years old; he took over management of the family property, but he fared no better than his debt-ridden father.

In 1876, therefore, George Hearst bought the Santa Rosa prop-

Sebastian's store originally served the whalers that worked out of the bay of San Simeon; now moved to another site, it continues to serve the village of San Simeon as a general store.

Padron by James Walker. This painting, together with its companion piece reproduced on the opposite page, was made by an Englishman who traveled from Mexico to New York to South America, and eventually to California, where he settled in 1884. These portraits of the proprietor of a major California ranch and one of his *vaqueros* are authentic in every detail.

Vaquero by James Walker |

Don "Pancho" Estrada, who taught four generations of Hearsts to ride. Photographed in his eighties, he appeared as the Grand Marshall of parades in California, sparkling with silver on his costume, his saddle, and his horse.

erty and the young owner, Pancho Estrada, went to work for the Hearst family, where he remained for his lifetime. Pancho was only a few years older than George's only son, but he was always in charge of the personal riding horses and acted as riding instructor and companion, first to George's son William Randolph and then to William's sons and even his grandsons. Senator George Hearst instructed his son, Willie, to speak respectfully and to address Estrada as "Don," the Spanish title of respect. Willie in turn gave his own five sons the same orders, which were passed down to John Hearst, George Hearst's great grandson. Don Pancho, who supervised the riding horses for four generations of Hearsts, lived in the village of San Simeon in a house built for him by the Hearsts overlooking the bay. Since his family had been owners of the original ranches, he was a living symbol of the history of San Simeon. His grandfather and father had been citizens of three countries: Spain, Mexico, and finally the United States.

Part II/Mountains of Gold

Chapter 4/George Hearst, Gold Miner

Comes Traveller and his master [Lee].
...Such horses are
The jewels of the horseman's hands and
thighs,
They go by the word and hardly need
the rein.
They bred such horses in Virginia then,
Horses that were remembered after
death
And buried not so far from Christian
ground....

—Stephen Vincent Benét

*I*n 1850, George Hearst left Franklin County, Missouri, on horseback. He was thirty years old and had saved up his money to buy a fine horse and hoped to join a group of covered wagons heading West. His mother and sister rode with him for the first two days, and as they turned back, they waved goodbye until he was out of sight. By the time he returned in 1861, his sister had died and his mother would be on her deathbed.

But now he was heading out, full of hope, to California and mountains of gold. Thousands would die in the attempt but when Hearst got to the gold fields, he was better prepared than most. Missouri had many lead mines, one of them only a mile from his late father's farm. For several years, young George had determined that the mining of lead could be improved. He learned a lot about mining and believed that if the mines were operated more economically and efficiently, they could make more money. So he gave more time to mining and less to running the farm.

In 1846, the same year that the Mexican flag was replaced with the American in faraway California, George's father, William, had died $10,000 in debt, leaving a courageous widow, Elizabeth, a twenty-six-year-old son, George, a teen-age daughter, Martha (Patsy), and a crip-
California Bound by
Sam Savitt
pled son, Philip, to run the farm. George had to work his heart out to provide for them.

A neighboring family, the Appersons from Virginia, were comforting and helpful. As close friends and distant cousins, the Appersons had named their little girl, Phoebe Elizabeth, for George's mother, Elizabeth Collins Hearst. George would often ride over to the Appersons, pick up his mother's namesake, and take her back on his horse to visit his mother.

Another neighbor, Dr. Silas Reed, owned a lead mine and lent young George many books on geology and mining. Lead had been mined in Missouri since 1719 and the mineral continued to be in demand for firearms. Soon young George leased some lead claims. He worked them according to his own ideas of improved methods and made enough money between 1846 and 1849 to pay off his father's debts and to buy a few comforts for his mother and sister, Patsy. (The crippled brother, Philip, had died.)

With the debts paid off, George Hearst felt that his family were safe. Like thousands of others in Missouri, he was attracted to flashes of gold in California. He was ready to move on, to join the wagon trains rumbling West, to make his fortune. George Hearst had never been further away from home in his whole life than forty miles, the distance to the nearest city, St. Louis, where he went to outfit himself for the long ride to California. His cousins and closest friends, Joseph and Jacob Clark, were going West, too, along with eight other men and six women from the same neighborhood.

The day before he left, he rode over to the Appersons' farm again to ask them to look after his mother and sister, to say goodbye and to give little Phoebe Elizabeth, nicknamed Puss, one last ride on his horse. Her eyes filled with tears.

"Don't cry Puss, like a papoose," he scolded her. "I'll bring you a nice present from California." Deep in his heart, however, he realized he might never come back.

The others in Hearst's party had started ahead in prairie schooners, but Hearst and a young neighbor named Phillips expected they could catch up in a few days with some hard riding.

His last view of the fields he had harvested, of the Meramac River where he had learned to swim, and of the hills, made him sad. Years later he said that he still remembered the powerful temptation he felt to turn back to the land he had grown up on, the world he loved. But still he turned his horse to the West!

Hearst and Phillips rode first through the rolling hills of Missouri into Kansas which was then called "Indian Country." They reached the Santa Fé Trail, a covered-wagon road where many caravans were now heading West. For some miles Hearst and his friend would ride with a wagon group, then they would head off, alone by day, hoping to camp with a group of wagons at night for companionship, safety, and the good food prepared over campfires by the women.

Senator George Hearst,
1820–1891

Everyone hoped to reach the Sierras before snowfall, remembering what had happened when the Donner party had been lost in those mountains in the winter of 1846. The wagons were pulled slowly, hitched to horses, mules, or oxen. They became stuck in the mud and forded dangerous rivers; they were watched by Indians and sickened by cholera, but still they slogged on, ever westward. Crossing the Kansas River by ferry, the wagons were hauled onto boats, while the oxen and horses were forced to swim. Hearst and Phillips traveled hard to catch up with their own party. At one lonely post office along the route, they found a message nailed to a post:

WE WANT TO BE IN CALIFORNIA BEFORE
THE SNOW. DON'T DELAY. PLEASE HURRY.
JOE CLARK

And hurry they did. Whenever he could George wrote and sent home letters and messages to his mother, telling her he was safe, probably not mentioning his bout with cholera and the fact that fever, chill, and delirium had held them up a few more days.

At one river swollen by storms, they hesitated before plunging in. Suddenly a little red-headed boy jumped in and led them over. Hearst never forgot that boy. "If it hadn't been for him, that red-headed boy," George enjoyed recounting in later years, "I never would have gotten to the West." But Hearst and Phillips endured the storms, the dust and sand, the thirst and hunger, the cholera and the earthshaking herds of buffalo. They made it over mountains, deserts, rivers, and prairies. Just beyond Fort Kearney, at a pure spring near the post office of Ash Hollow, they found their friends' wagons in camp. Hearst and his cousin, Joe Clark, rushed into each other's arms with whoops of joy.

In spite of the triumphs, tragedy trudged along that trail to California as well. Oxen died, crippled horses were shot, and young and old alike succumbed to illness. The graves of men, women, and children were marked along the way with forlorn little wooden crosses. Still, there were good moments on the trail as they sang "Oh Suzannah" and their beloved hymns, as they huddled around the campfires. To the end of his days, George Hearst would remain a man of that rough trail, of the plains, the desert, the mountains, and the great, open sky.

As soon as he got to California in 1851, a year after he started out, Hearst knew the arduous trip had been worth it. He knew he would become a millionaire. He soon located a ledge of gold on the line that divided Grass Valley and Nevada City. He named his mine Merrimac, varying the spelling slightly from the river Meramac back home in Missouri. He filed legal papers for his claim, formed a company, and set to work. In 1852 he found another mine which he called the Potosi after a lead mine he had known well in Missouri.

It was with the Merrimac and Potosi mines that Hearst made his first big money, although he located, prospected, developed, and sold many other mines, working with his cousins, the Clarks. A really big find would be made in a part of Nevada then called Utah, 160 miles from Sacramento over the Sierra Nevada, down to the town of Carson in the region known by its Indian name of Wasseau, later Washoe. The gold and silver in that area became known throughout the world as the Comstock Lode. From his experience in lead mines, Hearst knew that the strange black ore found there along with the gold was not lead, but silver.

Hearst had been one of the first to arrive in the gold hills of the Comstock Lode country, later Virginia City, Nevada. He bought a one-sixth interest in the Ophir mine for $3,000, one of the first claims

Phoebe Apperson
Hearst, 1844–1919

Came to America
with Dr. Thomas Clark and his shipload of
Presbyterian-Scots in May, 1764 from Bally Vay,
will written 9 Sept. 1780, Long Cane Dist., South Ca...

JOHN HEA...

ROBERT H.   GEORGE H.   JOHN H. = MARTHA CARSON   THOMAS H.   JOSEPH H. = JAN...
D. 1806   *dau. of William and*   *Probably born*   Si...
M. 2 PHOEBE STARK   *Margaret Carson... her sister*   *in Ireland*
Major in Continental   M. *Capt. Josiah Patterson of Abbeville*   *Private in Revolutionary...*
Army

WILLIAM H.   JOHN H. = SARAH WARDLAW
D.S.P.   B.1757~D.1843   *dau of John Wardlaw*

Dr. JOHN WARDLAW H = ANN CHILES
B. 1813 ~ D. 1878   *dau of Joh...*
D.S.P.

MARGARET H.   ROBERT H.   WILLIAM G.H. = ELIZABETH COLLINS   MARY H. = JACOB CLARK Jr.
B. 6 Sept., 1772   B. 22 Aug., 1774   B. 1776, Woodville Dist. S.C.   B. S.Car. dau. of Jacob   B. 4 Oct. 1778   *son of Jacob Cl...*
    Moved to Franklin Co., Mo.   *and Martha (Coleman) Collins*   (B. 1765 ~ D.22
    D2. 1817   *sister of Anna who m. Austin Clark*   *and Anne Livings...*
                                  (B. 1744)

JOHN FAVOR = ISABEL RANDOLPH
MARTHA H.   PHILIP H.   JOHN FAVOR = ANN COVINGTON *dau of*   PHILOMEN KAVANAUGH
Died young   *Thomas and Joel Kavanaugh*
    FRANCIS APPERSON = ELIZABETH LONG   *originally GEORGE FRIED W...*
    B. Carolina Co., Va. ~ a Culpeper Co., Va.   *changed to GEORGE FREDERICK W...*
     Dr. JOHN APPERSON = ALICEY FAVOR   B. Switzerland, Wirtem berg, Ger. To
     B. 1763, Culpeper Co., Va.   B. 10 April 1767, Culpeper Co., Va.   *Philadelphia about the*
     D. Sept.1855 Franklin Co.   D. Dec.1856, Louisville, Clay Co., Ill.   M. PHOEBE HAPGOO...
         M. 29 Jan., 1844   HENRY WHIT...
    RANDOLPH WALKER APPERSON = DRUSILLA WHITMIRE   B. 22 John New Ge...
    B. 10 Apr., 1800, Washington Co.,Ky   B. 24 Sept. 1816, Newbury, S.C.   D. 5 Feb., 1936
    D. 17 Nov. 1900, Santa Clara, Cal.   D. 1885, Franklin Co., Mo.   ELBERT CLARK APPERSON
                  M. 15 June, 1863   B. 30 Jan. 1851, Dent Co. Mo.

Went to California   GEORGE HEARST = PHOEBE ELIZABETH APPERSON   ANN DRUCILLA A.   RAN...
in Gold Rush   B. 3 Sept., 1820, Franklin Co. Mo.   B. 3 Dec., 1842, Franklin Co., Mo.   B. 20 April 1878
     D. 28 Feb., 1891, Washington, D.C.   D. 22 Jan., 1919.   M. Dr. JOSEPH MARSHALL FLINT
     Died while Representative from   *Founded National Cathedral*   WILLIAM WALKE...
     California in Senate 1886 to 1891   *School P.T.A. (Washington, D.C.)*   FL...
                        Benefactor to Mt. Vernon   GEORGE WILLSO...

Member of Congress from New York   WILLIAM RANDOLPH HEARST = MILLICENT WILLSON
Founder of the "Hearst Empire"   B. 29 April, 1863, San Francisco, Calif.   B. 1881, New York
     D. 14 Aug. 1951, Los Angeles, Calif.   D. Dec. 1974, New York

GEORGE RANDOLPH H.   WILLIAM RANDOLPH H. Jr.   JOHN RANDOLPH ...
B. 23 April, 1904, Washington, D.C.   *Publisher~Editor..Awarded the Pulitzer Prize*   B. 1910 ~ D. 1958
D. 1972   B. 27 Jan., 1908, New York, N.Y.   M. D. GRETCHEN W...
M. BLANCHE LILLIAN WILBUR   M. 29 July, 1948, Warrenton, Va.   M. 2 DEANNE WA...
B. 19 June, 1902   AUSTINE BYRNE McDONNELL
Idaho Falls, Idaho   B. 22 Nov., 1928, Newtown, Mass.
       dau. of Major Austin McCarthy McDonnell,
       and Mary Theresa Bett, 17 Nov. 1927, Warrenton, Va.

   WILLIAM RANDOLPH H III   JOHN AUGUSTINE CHILTON H
   B. 18 July, 1949, Washington, D.C.   B. 24 Oct. 1952, Washington, D.C.
   M. NAN PELETZ   M. 1 July, 1984
   B. 16 Aug., 1949, San Francisco   CHRISTINE B. MULARCHUK
   dau. of Cyril Morton and Shirley Anne (Gates) Peletz   B. 1952
                            dau. of Margaret Peterson and
                            Peter G. Mularchuk

GEORGE RANDOLPH H. Jr.   PHOEBE H.
B. 1927   B. 1927
M. MARY THOMPSON   M. 1 PHILIP TOVREA
B. 23 March, 1931,   M. 2 AMORY COOKE
Sarasota, Fla.   (1)
         PHOEBE TOVREA   WILLIAM RANDOLPH H. IV   ADELAIDE APPERSON H.
         B. 31 Mar. 1952, Phoenix, Ariz.   B. 2 May, 1979, Los Angeles, Calif.   B. 4 July, 1983, San Francisco Cal.
                                                   JOHN R.
MARY H.   GEORGE RANDOLPH H.   STEPHEN H.   ERIN H.   B. 8 Dec.
B. 8 Apr. 1953   B. Feb. 1955   B. 18 Sept., 1956   B. 6 June, 1959   M. D. 3 ...
M. D. LON E. STEIN   M. CHRISTINE STERGE   M. ARMON LEE GEAR   PATRICIA
M. D. Dr. BRUCE   B. 8 June, 1952   D. 1984   M. 2) 16
W. EDWARDS   KATHLE...
B. 2 Oct., 1948

         (1)   (2)   LISA TENNY H.   JOHN HE...
   SHANNON MARIE S.   ALEXIS APPERSON S.   B. 27 April, 1963   B. 1961
   B. 22 Sept., 1972   B. 23 Aug., 1974

The Hearst Family Tree |

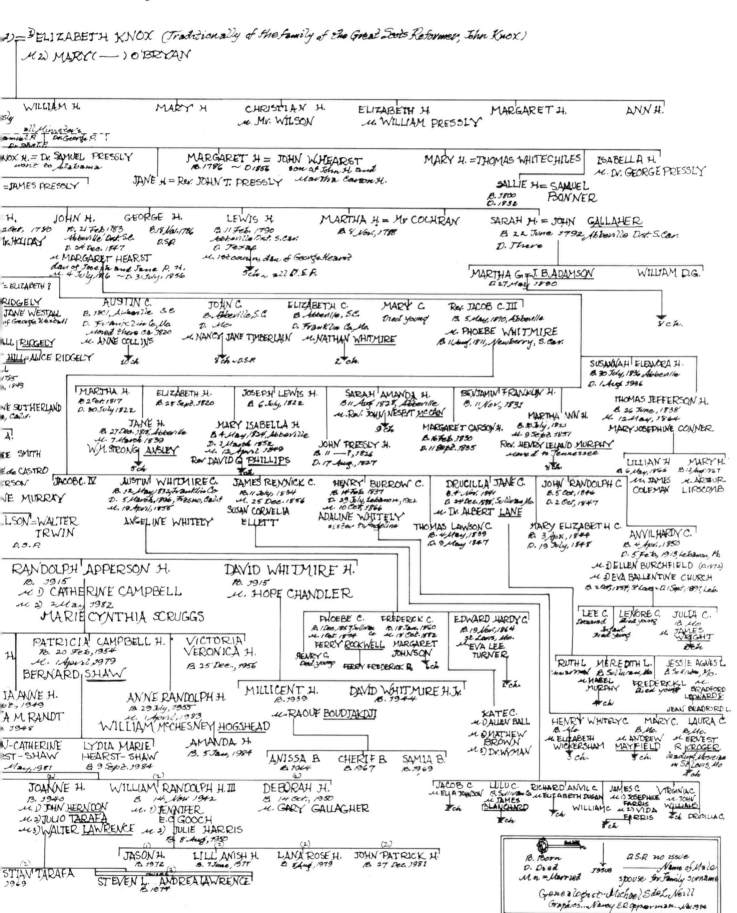

HEARST Family of Scotland, Virginia, Missouri, and California

1) = Elizabeth KNOX (Traditionally of the family of the Great Scots Reformer, John Knox)
M 2) MARY (——) O'BRYAN

WILLIAM H.   MARY H.   CHRISTIAN H. m. Mr. WILSON   ELIZABETH H. m. WILLIAM PRESSLY   MARGARET H.   ANN H.

all Minister's

NOX H. = Dr. SAMUEL PRESSLY went to Alabama

MARGARET H. = JOHN W. HEARST B.1786 ~ D.1856 son of John H. and Martha Carson H.

JANE H. = Rev. JOHN T. PRESSLY

MARY H. = THOMAS WHITECHILES

SALLIE H. = SAMUEL BONNER B.1800 D.1832

ISABELLA H. m. Dr. GEORGE PRESSLY

= JAMES PRESSLY

H. JOHN H. GEORGE H. LEWIS H. MARTHA H. = Mr COCHRAN SARAH H. = JOHN GALLAHER

MARTHA G. = J.B.ADAMSON D.27 May 1890

WILLIAM D.G.

AUSTIN C. JOHN C. ELIZABETH C. MARY C. Died young Rev. JACOB C. III m. PHOEBE WHITMIRE

SUSANNAH ELEANORA H.

THOMAS JEFFERSON H.

MARY JOSEPHINE CONNER

MARTHA H. ELIZABETH H. JOSEPH LEWIS H. SARAH AMANDA H. BENJAMIN FRANKLIN H.

LILLIAN H. MARY H.

RANDOLPH APPERSON H. DAVID WHITMIRE H.

PATRICIA CAMPBELL H. VICTORIA VERONICA H.

JOANNE H. WILLIAM RANDOLPH H. III DEBORAH H.

81

recorded in the area. To pay for it, he sold part of his other claims and borrowed some from a local hotel keeper. Another claim in the vicinity in which he bought a share became The Gould and Curry Silver Mining Company. On June 25, 1860, four feet of that claim went to each of twelve incorporators, among whom were George Hearst, Lloyd Tevis, John Earl, William Blanding, and William Ralston. All twelve men became millionaires many times over.

Built in 1860 in Virginia City, Nevada, for the Gould and Curry Silver Mining Company, this house was lived in first by George Hearst and later by his mine manager, John Mackay.

By this time, George was considered lucky. Wherever he went, gold and silver turned up. In the bitter winter of 1859, he took a load of his ore down the mountains by mule train and then traveled by riverboat all the way to San Francisco. He wanted to find experts not available in the high country to extract, assay, and appraise the ore. When it proved to be very rich in silver, Hearst and his partners were jubilant.

At this time, however, a letter came that changed his plans. Throughout the ten years he was away, Hearst had written faithfully to his mother and sister. But now his mother wrote urging him to return. His sister, Patsy, had died and his mother confessed that she herself was gravely ill. In haste, George sold part of his mine and made plans to leave immediately for Missouri. During the winter of 1861 he arrived at his mother's bedside and visited with his former neighbors, cousins, and friends. They marvelled at his stories and at the gold nuggets he had brought with him.

The graceful, gray-eyed little girl he had left, Phoebe Elizabeth Apperson, was now seventeen, a graceful, gray-eyed young woman, who had been kind to his ill mother. She could play the piano, speak French, and ride a horse. She was fragile, bright, and pretty as porcelain, not at all like the rough women he had met in the gold fields. Phoebe and he often rode together that winter, sometimes for long distances without speaking. They were happy in each other's company. His mother smiled, understood, and was delighted. Phoebe's parents liked George but thought he was too old for their schoolteacher daughter, who was not yet eighteen. When Hearst came to call they were cool.

One day in spring his mother looked up at him from her sickbed and whispered, "George, I will meet you in Heaven." Those were her last words. After George buried her beside his father, his brother, and his sister, he decided it was time to go back to his mines and to California. In spite of her family's protests, George and Phoebe were married in June of 1862, and in September of that year the bride and groom left for New York to sail to the Isthmus of Panama. After crossing Panama by horseback and mule train, they took a boat to San Francisco.

A family legend recounts that Phoebe knew her husband was a miner and that he had done well, but she did not know he was a millionaire. Before leaving home she bought a piece of brown merino wool to make into a dress on the long way to California. The story goes that upon reaching San Francisco George ordered for her first a black, rustling silk dress trimmed with lace and then many bright, fashionable silk dresses, one after another. A lady friend to whom Phoebe complained of her husband's wild extravagances told her, "Don't worry, dear. Your husband is part owner in one of the richest mines of the West."

Hearst accumulated more and more gold. More mines in Utah, in the Black Hills of the Dakotas. Under his touch, everything turned to gold or silver. At the mines and in Virginia City, Hearst met and dealt with men who would become rich, powerful, and famous. One of them, Samuel Clemens, was a fellow Missourian and the two men called each other by their first names. Clemens, pen-named Mark Twain, loved to tell a story about Hearst and a new starched shirt. Apparently Hearst had saved such a shirt in his Virginia City hotel room for a banquet they were both attending. Clemens had no white "biled" shirt, so he "happened" into Hearst's room that evening and borrowed the one Hearst had reserved. When he later pointed out to friends how he had worn the starched white shirt while Hearst had to wear an ordinary one, Hearst answered quick as a wink, "That's so, Sam. And it's the only time you were ever well dressed in your life."

Hearst and his bride moved into a handsome mansion in San Francisco, and as their fortune increased, their family increased with the birth of their son, named William for George's father, and Randolph for Phoebe's father. Mrs. Hearst hated to leave the baby, but she often accompanied her husband on visits to Virginia City and the other mining towns. The cultural opportunities and the social activities of San Francisco also kept her busy. George loved his horses and the races, and he decided the time had come to invest his gold. He would put the gold he took from the land, back into land, land in their new state of California.

Chapter 5/Stagecoach Horses West

It was the stage-driver's story,
   as he stood with his back to the wheelers,
Quietly flecking his whip and turning his
      quid of tobacco,
While on the dusty road, and blent with
      the rays of the moonlight,
We saw the lash of his whip and the juice
      of tobacco descending....

—Bret Harte

*A*lthough not every miner who did well in California turned his money into land and well-bred horses, George Hearst was not alone. Other miners, including Theodore Winters and Leland Stanford, shared his enthusiasm and his determination to improve the Thoroughbred horse. No one knows exactly—and Hearst never said—why he loved horses so much, but it is not surprising when you remember that the entire world in the middle of the nineteenth century was dependent for many things—including power and transportation—on horses. In the eastern United States, as in Europe, the industrial revolution had enabled man to rely on machines, and it would not be many years before railroad trains and "horseless carriages" would replace horses as part of everyday life (though the engines would continue to be rated in terms of "horsepower"!). But in the old West, much of which was still a little-explored frontier, horses were crucial to existence. It may be that progressive men like George Hearst saw enough into the future to determine that the beautiful horse might soon be relegated to a symbolic rather than a practical importance and that he chose to champion their cause and celebrate their contribution to American history by raising the most beautiful specimens of the breed.

Horses had been an integral part of the history of California ever since the arrival of the Spanish. At isolated San Simeon, for example, communication with the rest of the world depended on horses. Horses were the only means of travel and transport; they brought letters, parcels, medicines, and what few luxuries there were.

The Stagecoach Heading for San Luis Obispo by Sam Savitt

During the first years of Spanish colonization the California missions relied on ships from Mexico to deliver mail and supplies to the

The Overland Mail Company, Barlow, Sanderson & Co. (artist unknown). The Overland Mail Company was organized to conduct the express business between New York and San Francisco via the Isthmus of Panama. One of the founders was William G. Fargo, who founded American Express in 1850 and, with Henry Wells, the Wells Fargo Company in 1852; Wells Fargo purchased the Overland Mail Company in 1866.

bays where they would be landed in smaller boats and then transported inland by riders or horse-drawn wagons. Urgent messages were sometimes carried on horseback by couriers and soldiers from one ranch or *presidio* ("fort") to the next. Roads from ranch to ranch were simple Indian tracks, best traveled on horseback. Inns were few, so a courier would stop at the ranches for meals, staying for hours, days, weeks, no matter. He would usually be given a fresh horse which he could drop off at the next ranch. Or someone would ride with the traveler to the next ranch and bring back the borrowed horse.

W. G. Dana, a cousin of Richard Dana, author of *Two Years Before the Mast*, wrote of the Spanish horsemen:

> *The men appeared to always be on horseback. There are probably no better riders in the world ... the stirrups are covered, or boxed, up in front to prevent their catching when they are riding in the woods; and the saddles are hard and heavy ... have large pommels ... they make no use of the stirrups in mounting, but striking the horse, spring into the saddle as he trots ... Their spurs are cruel things, having four or five rowels, each an inch in length ... the flanks of the horses are often bloody from them.*

After California and San Simeon became a part of the United States, the horse and the ship were still the only ways the government could send mail, or the private citizen could get supplies or transportation. Travelers and settlers from the eastern United States came by boat to the Isthmus of Panama, across the Isthmus by packhorse, and then by ship again up the Pacific Coast. That was the way Phoebe Apperson Hearst had traveled to California with her bridegroom. Only a few years later the steamer *Golden Age* would sail into San Francisco Bay with passengers after only twenty-two days at sea from New York to San Francisco, the fastest journey ever. Settlers heading for California from the middle regions of the United States usually traveled in prairie schooners rather than ships, the big Conestoga wagons drawn by horses, mules, or oxen.

The first overland San Simeon mail contract was obtained in 1868 by the Sheriff of San Luis Obispo County, J. P. Lewelling. He operated his first regular mail and passenger runs each Saturday from San Simeon to San Luis Obispo. Crude wagons were used to bring the mail and to bounce passengers on rough, dusty rides in the summer and muddy rides in the winter. Anyone who had a choice would choose to ride a horse or take a private buggy. Sheriff Lewelling could not tolerate the daily grind and so he sold out before a year was up to a new owner, who himself sold out within a year to an experienced driver of stagecoaches, a Mr. G. S. Miller.

Miller contracted for mail delivery and ran his stage three times a week from Cambria, a town near San Simeon. The stage left at seven in the morning, traveled forty miles to San Luis Obispo, and arrived by three the same afternoon. Stages left on Friday, Monday, and Wednesday; and on Saturday, Tuesday, and Thursday they made the return trip. The fare was $3 for a one-way passage, no small amount in those days. The road, only a track in most places, crossed privately owned homesteads or grants; the main roads centered at the missions, San Antonio, San Luis Obispo, and San Miguel. North of San Simeon there was no road, only a sand path for a few miles to the Piedra Blanca lighthouse.

Between San Luis Obispo and San Simeon the road meandered across streams, along pastures, and over hills. One brave traveler who journeyed out to San Simeon wrote in the San Luis Obispo newspaper, "The road is as good as it ever was, once you get down to it."

A local newspaper editor complained, "Our coast from San Luis Obispo to Piedra Blanca is peculiarly situated. To travel conveniently from *any* of its points to San Francisco, it is necessary to go south to San Luis Obispo and then take a stage or a ship north."

In order to visit their ranch from their home in San Francisco, the George Hearsts took a boat to San Luis Obispo's harbor called Avila where a buggy would meet them. The land trip was roughly (and I mean rough!) fifty miles. A midway change of horses would be arranged for the trip, which lasted an entire day from seven in the morning until late afternoon.

After her husband's death, Phoebe often made the trip alone. Her coachman, Cipriano Soto, was descended from a well-known military family of Monterey. His father, Yrculano Soto, born in 1832 in Monterey, had first settled land around the Mission San Antonio at Jolon, which generations later would become the property of W. R. Hearst, George's son. Soto moved his family again to a ranch in the mountains near the hamlet of Adelaida, behind San Simeon. One of five sons, Cipriano, eventually became the coachman for Mrs. Hearst. It was his son, Andrew, and his daughter who told me how their father would hitch up horses at the San Simeon Ranch carriage house, drive half a day, stop halfway, change horses to a borrowed team, and continue to San Luis Obispo to spend the night. The next day, Mrs. Hearst, who had spent the night there after her boat trip, would be picked up at eight in the morning. The carriage would stop again en route to return the borrowed horses and pick up the original team to carry them the rest of the way to remote San Simeon.

The public stage line and the United States Mail contract were sold again in 1871. The operators this time were a Mr. Brown and a Mr. Castro, the same pair who lived on the original Piedra Blanca grant and who now owned a livery stable. The two men added newer, larger coaches and fast horses. A coach left every day from the town of Cambria, near San Simeon.

But Mrs. Hearst had far too many trunks to take the passenger coach. Members of the Soto family have recounted the story of how she would bring many trunks of presents, "whether it was Christmas or no," to every person who worked on the ranch and to each child of every family. Besides, on the public stages, a lady might meet a rough-and-tumble lot of passengers, not to mention the gun-toting drivers.

Those stagecoach drivers, along with the Indians, the bandits, and buffalos, were the legends of the West, and with good reason. Stagecoach drivers were admired much as airline pilots are today, and, with few exceptions, they too were sober, talented, and tough.

In the book *Stagecoaching on El Camino Real*, coaching historian Charles Outland writes: "In the process of searching through forty years of newspaper files this writer never found one instance wherein a stagecoach driver was accused of drinking."

As railway lines expanded, stagecoaching had decreased greatly in the East and Midwest, so that the last long-distance equine transportation system was only in the West. In California stagecoaches traveled over rutted roads, deserts, and mountains, transporting the newly rich gold miners and bringing them the mail, the necessities, and the luxuries they could afford. These coaches, drawn by six- or four-horse teams, were driven by the most seasoned, expert reinsmen.

The names Hank Monk, Charley Baker, and "One-Eyed" Charley Parkhurst are justly celebrated in literature as the drivers of the California Coast Line Stages. Standing about 5 feet 7 inches tall, Charley Parkhust smoked and chewed tobacco, rolled dice, played cards, and took an occasional drink, but never used profanity (unlike most reinsmen). He was blue eyed, broad shouldered, and had a smooth, sun-browned face and a high-pitched voice. Charley was considered the safest, fastest driver in California. An invitation to ride on the box with One-Eyed Charley was an honor for J. Ross Brown, a California writer in the 1860s. The trip resulted in an article in a newspaper:

> *It was 5 o'clock p.m. when we took our places … I had implicit confidence in old Charley. The way he handled the reins and peered through clouds of dust and volumes of darkness and saw trees and stumps and boulders of rock, and horses' ears, when I could scarcely see my own hand before me, was a miracle of stage driving.*
>
> *"Git aeoup!," was the warning cry of this old stager. "Git alang, my beauties!" …*
>
> *"How in the world can you see your way?"*
>
> *"Smell it! Fact is, I've traveled over these mountains so often I can tell where the road is by the sound of the wheels. When they rattle I'm on hard ground. When they don't rattle I genr'ly look over the sides to see where she's a going."*

No highwayman held up the stage with Charley on the box in

more than thirty years, not since the first two had tried and he shot them dead. When Charley died after his retirement, kind neighbors prepared the body for burial and discovered that the greatest stage driver of the West had actually been a woman. A doctor's examination established that Charley had also been a mother.

As today's airline pilots must handle hijackers, the stage drivers had to operate their vehicles and at the same time cope with hijackers, drunken passengers, highway robbers, and nervous horses. Horses can be unpredictable. A quail or a feather may flutter across their paths and away they will go, hooves flying.

In the Ventura newspaper of 1876, we read:

> *On Monday, the dawn stage from Santa Barbara with four passengers upset ... The horses were scared by the falling dirt from above the grade and shied, taking the stage off the embankment ... Mr. McCarty [the driver] informed us that the stage turned over three times ... Serious injuries were not inflicted."*

On another occasion we read in the *Ventura Free Press* that "the driver was assisting passengers to alight for breakfast when the horses became frightened and ran away, with Miss Annie Wagner and two children inside. The team dashed down the grade and up the next hill, when the occupants found an opportunity to jump out."

The first rule was that the driver should never leave his horses unattended, and with four or six horses, he should securely tie the leaders. Driving a single team, the driver would drop the inside traces from the doubletree and tie the reins extra tight.

The Ventura *Signal* of 1875 tells how "the lead horses were precipitated down an embankment 150 feet and killed, and the passengers and coach had a narrow escape." Or again, on another stage, "the horses became unmanageable and the stage went over the bank down to the bottom of the canyon, a distance of 200 feet. The driver and passengers jumped off uninjured. Two horses were killed."

Outpost stagecoach stops for changing horses were targets for horse thieves, and California had more horse thieves than Boston had beans. I have been told that the little remodeled cottage, built about 1871, where we stay at Pico Creek on the Hearst ranch, was a stagecoach stop on the road to San Luis Obispo. As far as I know, however, our stagecoach stop was too small and out of the way to have been frequented by the likes of Tiburcio Vasquez who was robbing stagecoaches and stealing horses in the county around 1874.

Most stage lines had two types of stops, located every ten or fifteen miles. Manned by stock tenders, a blacksmith, and other burly types, often fugitives from the law, the small stop consisted of a stable, a supply of feed, perhaps eight horses, and a couple of rooms for the staff. The larger home station had stabling for perhaps twenty horses and a coach repair shop, as well as a blacksmith and sleeping and dining accommodations for travelers and drivers. Some stations were even equipped to grow their own hay.

Stagecoach horses were well fed, fat, sleek, and fast, often leaving their stations at a full gallop, settling down later into a rapid trot. The coaches were sturdy and the men who drove them were sturdier still.

The train whistle blowing in the distance didn't silence the rattle of the Concord Coach or the buggy and farm wagon out at San Simeon. Those rocking vehicles and their steel-nerved drivers may have wheeled into the sunset elsewhere in the West, like the herds of buffalo. San Simeon, however, continued to depend on the horse, until 1915 and the coming of the motor car.

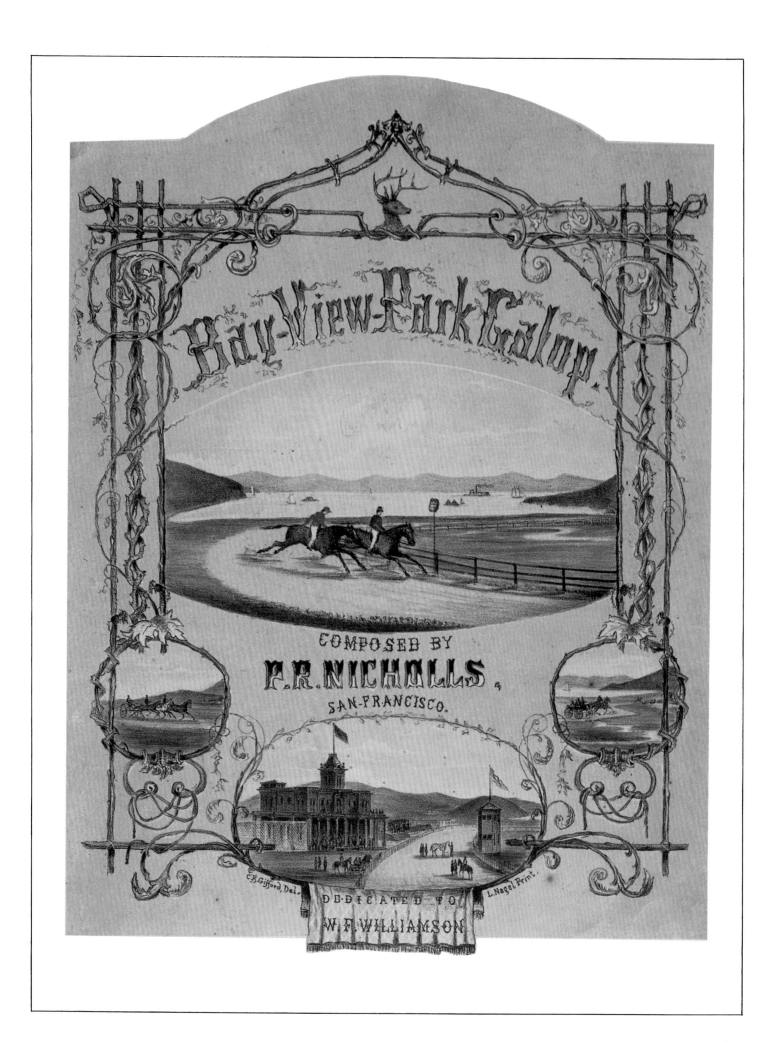

Bay-View-Park Galop.

COMPOSED BY

F. R. NICHOLLS,

SAN-FRANCISCO.

C.B.Gifford, Del.

L.Nagel Print.

DEDICATED TO

W. F. WILLIAMSON

Chapter 6/George Hearst's Thoroughbred Racehorses

A horse! a horse!
my kingdom for a horse!

—William Shakespeare

*L*ike George Hearst, his friends and business partners, James Ben Ali Haggin, Leland Stanford, Theodore Winters, Elias Jackson "Lucky" Baldwin, Marcus Daly, and Jim Fair, were interested in land and livestock, especially Thoroughbred horses. Horse breeding and horse racing were fun for those daredevil, gold-plated, new-rich mining men.

Horse racing in California had begun soon after the first Spanish soldiers rode in. One hundred and forty horses came with the commander of the first land expedition into Alta California, and Captain Rivera y Moncado and his twenty-five mounted soldiers in leather armor probably entertained themselves in off-duty hours by racing their horses. Hernando Cortés, the conqueror of Mexico, had allowed his men to enjoy the sport. A member of Cortés's army, Señor Bernal Diaz, kept a journal in which he detailed various mares and stallions and their racing abilities.

The *macho* Spanish, justly proud of their horses and their horsemanship, invariably improvised a racecourse on any level stretch of land or beach. A racecourse at the Pueblo of Los Angeles followed what is now Pico Street for four miles, ending at the present intersection of Pico and Main Streets. San Francisco's racetrack was near the Mission Dolores and the settlements of Santa Barbara, San Diego, San Luis Obispo, and Monterey all had racetracks as well.

"The dance and a dashing horse are the two objects which overpower all others with interest for all Californians," observed Walter Colton, a Protestant clergyman who arrived in Monterey in 1846 as Chaplain of the frigate commanded by Commodore Stockton. Colton spent three years there and was appointed as first mayor, or *alcalde*, by Commodore Stockton; later when martial law ended, he was elected to

In 1863 George Hearst directed the construction of the Bay View Park racetrack in what is now the Butchertown section of San Francisco. The decorative cover of this sheet music, drawn by C. R. Gifford, shows the club house, the judges' stand, and the racehorses both galloping and trotting against a backdrop of San Francisco Bay.

From JIM BROWN in 1881 to DR. ROSS in 1891, many of George Hearst's horses won at the old Oakland course near San Francisco.

Previous page: *Tournament Wins at Sheepshead Bay* by Sam Savitt. George Hearst's greatest racehorse, TOURNAMENT, won the Realization Stakes at the Coney Island Jockey Club's Sheepshead Bay course on July 2, 1890.

that post. Eventually he would found California's first newspaper.

Colton returned east in 1849, obviously amazed at the stamina of California's horses of Andalusian ancestry. In a book he wrote of a long ride taken by John C. Fremont and his friend Don Pico, owner of the Piedra Blanca ranch. The ride started in Los Angeles and went not only to San Luis Obispo but beyond there to Monterey. Eight-hundred-and-forty miles in seventy-six hours.

"The two horses ridden by the Colonel ... were a present to him from Don Jesus," wrote the Reverend Colton, and he explained that the horses were, "brothers, one a year younger than the other, both the same color ... cinnamon and hence called EL CANELO."

Those cinnamon-colored horses that carried Fremont to Monterey and, after one night's rest, back to San Luis Obispo, must have been the horses of the same name that had won races for Don Pico and had been given by him to Fremont. Whether Fremont took one of these horses to San Francisco and sold him or left him with Pico is still debated by historians of horse racing.

EL CANELO's blood with all its staying power may have flowed in some of the early trotters and pacers who raced in California in the 1820s. Their owners merely listed them "as part-Thoroughbreds, part-native-California stock."

A filly named CAMILLO URSO won the first running of the California Derby in 1873. Although registered in the Stud Book of Thoroughbreds, she was listed by Leland Stanford as a "trotting broodmare —sire unknown." Like many owners of the time, Senator Stanford clearly had some questions about the pedigree of his mare. The first Stud Book of American Racing Thoroughbreds was published in 1867 by J. H. Wallace but the author later admitted, "It began to dawn upon me that possibly I had been handling a great many fictions."

When the Spanish started racing in the 1760s, of course, there was no such horse as a registered Thoroughbred. Even in England the first Stud Book would not appear until 1791, and the General Stud Book would not be circulated until 1808. While Spanish soldiers were racing in the wilds of California, in England the greatest of Thoroughbred ancestors, ECLIPSE, was racing on Newmarket Heath, another natural flat site for a racetrack. Soon after that the new breed, the Thoroughbred, would travel from England to the New World.

By 1854 a number of these fast horses had come to California. First the Americans and then the Mexican-Americans caught the racing fever from these new Thoroughbred horses, which had sprung from

George Hearst's imported chestnut filly *GORGO, with jockey F. Littlefield in the irons, is being led to the starting post by trainer Matt Allen before winning the Siren Stakes for two-year-old fillies at the Sheepshead Bay course on September 4, 1888.

three founders, the GODOLPHIN ARABIAN, the BYERLY TURK, and the DARLEY ARABIAN. The supreme horse for racing, the horse of kings, the Thoroughbred has become a distinct breed in less than one hundred years. For all living Thoroughbreds descend from those three stallions who lived in the late seventeenth and early eighteenth centuries.

It is incredible that in the pedigree of an English horse named BAHRAM, who won the English triple crown in 1935, the name of the GODOLPHIN ARABIAN appeared 28,232 times, the BYERLY TURK 64,032 times and the DARLEY ARABIAN 44,079 times. Even a horse like little HYPERION (foaled 1930) shows up all over the globe in the bloodlines of horses from Hong Kong to Florida. Standing only 15.1 hands, bred by the seventeenth Earl of Derby, HYPERION has had more influence on the modern race horse than any other twentieth-century Thoroughbred. (The breed can range in size from 14 hands to 18 hands and comes in all colors except body-colored piebald, skewbald, dun, and Palomino.)

The first positively recorded Thoroughbred mare to reach California was BLACK SWAN, who was brought from Australia around 1852 by Don Andreas Sepulveda. She landed by sailing ship in San Francisco and walked to Los Angeles, where she beat former Governor Pio Pico's Spanish horse SARCO in a historic race.

Weighing the Jockeys
(artist unknown)

Inside the illustration:
THE MESSENGER BOY. BUY YOUR TICKETS ON THIS RACE
A WARMING UP GALLOP BEFORE A RACE
A NEW INSTITUTION PRINCIPALLY FOR THE USE OF SPORTING LADIES
REFRESHMENTS FOR THE GRAND STAND
CAPITAL THING! BEFORE RACES, WHEN USED WHICH BODY APPEARED TO BE THE CASE AT MONMOUTH.
THE FINISH. WHERE MANY A REPUTATION IS EITHER SHATTERED OR MADE.
GETTING READY FOR WORK.
ROLLING THE TRACK.
THE WATER JUMP. ALTAIR WINNER OF THE HANDICAP STEEPLECHASE.
BEFORE THE CONTEST HOODED AND ROBED LIKE A MONK.
NOTICES
THE TIME KEEPERS STAND
ON THE MEMBERS. STAND

Scenes and Incidents at Monmouth Park, 1884 (artist unknown). In 1888 at Monmouth Park in New Jersey, jockey F. Littlefield won on July 5 and August 4 riding *GORGO and SURINAM. In 1890 William Midgeley won aboard Hearst's RHONO and MISS BELL on July 26 and 29. That same year, on August 19 and 23, William Hayward rode TOURNAMENT to victory in the Omnibus and Delaware Handicaps, while on August 21, Anthony Hamilton finished first on RHONO.

Barry Whitehead, in an article published in *The Thoroughbred of California* in 1962, tells of the race between BLACK SWAN and SARCO. Apparently, the horses raced over a nine-mile cross-country course for a wager of one thousand head of cattle and several thousand dollars. The Thoroughbred mare won both the race and the admiration of California horse breeders. Large-scale Thoroughbred breeding got started soon after that race, for the Californians appreciated the "new" breed.

In 1854, three brothers named Williamson rode two mares and a Thoroughbred stallion, BELMONT, from Ohio to California. Not a Sunday passed in those days without horses being matched up in races near every large town in California.

In the year 1864, George Hearst put up the money to build one of the West's first and fastest major tracks, at Bay View Park at Butchertown, now part of San Francisco. As the city of San Francisco spread out, the racetracks had to move farther out. George Hearst, Leland Stanford, and others financed another track, called Oceanview, and yet another at the Bay District, out Gerry Boulevard. The Oceanview track put on the richest race in the world at that time, for a purse of $20,000 in gold. Hearst continued to support San Francisco racing throughout his

Brooklyn Handicap, Gravesend, May 14, 1887 by Henry Stull. Stull was the leading equestrian artist of the United States and Canada during the late nineteenth century and was much impressed with the photographs by Eadweard Muybridge, commissioned by George Hearst's colleague Leland Stanford, that showed the true movements of running horses. This painting of three horses at the finish line, one of them HIDALGO, ridden by Anthony Hamilton who would later become a contract jockey for Hearst, shows the accurate galloping

life. At the Bay District track on November 12, 1881, a mile race for two-year-olds who had not won at that distance was called the Hearst Stakes. George Hearst probably contributed the purse money.

By the second half of the nineteenth century, California had become one of the country's most important centers for the breeding of Thoroughbred horses. This was a remarkable development because, while everybody enjoyed racing in 1888, only five days of racing were scheduled for the spring meeting at San Francisco, and five more in the autumn. The major race meetings at Sacramento were also limited, and in Los Angeles, Fresno, Stockton, and San José, races were held only in connection with country fairs. California breeders, therefore, had to ship their horses East to race at the big tracks or to sell them to easterners.

In those days, horses were shipped by train. Crossing the mountains in those cold, windy boxcars was quite an ordeal. In 1888, *only one* railroad crossed the country by *only one* route—through the high Sierras. The trip was slow, and freight cars weren't heated, so that after the mild California climate, many an expensive horse got pneumonia. Many were lost, and all reached the East in poor condition. Still, the courageous Californians—remember, the mining men were gamblers—dared the journey. In spite of the obstacles, horses bred in California proved on the racetrack that they were the equal of horses bred in Kentucky and in other major horse-breeding centers.

Among the California breeders, Theodore Winters was a dominant figure for thirty years. His chief stallions were NORFOLK and JOE HOOKER. NORFOLK's story, you might say, began in England where Robert Aitcheson Alexander of Woodburn Farm, Woodford County, Kentucky, was traveling with his friend Richard Ten Broeck, owner of the Metairie Race Track near New Orleans. On that trip, Alexander bought the great six-year-old race horse LEXINGTON from his friend for $15,000.

Although LEXINGTON (by BOSTON out of ALICE CARNEAL by SARPEDON) was subsequently to become one of the greatest Thoroughbred sires in history, Mr. Alexander's neighbors in Kentucky considered $15,000 a ridiculously high price to pay for an untried stallion. The stallion's new owner, however, assured them that he would one day sell a son of LEXINGTON for more. He was right, because in 1864, he sold LEXINGTON's son NORFOLK, an unbeaten racehorse to Theodore Winters for $15,001. He had added the dollar, of course, to prove his point.

Winters' other major stallion, JOE HOOKER, was much less expensive. Carleton Burke, the first Californian to be elected a member of the Jockey Club in New York, described Winters' purchase of the horse as follows:

> *Driving along a country road near Willows, Calif., Theodore Winters saw a horse being led behind a covered wagon on the way to Oregon. The horse struck Winters' eye. He was obviously a Thoroughbred in fallen circumstances. Winters stopped the emigrants, examined the animal and bought him for a song. He learned the colt was a disgraced racer, barred from the tracks for roguishness and that his name was JOE HOOKER. Winters took the young stallion to his nearby ranch, gentled him, and put him to stud. He became a premier sire at Winters' Rancho del Rio and later at his new nursery, Rancho del Sierra near Carson City. JOE HOOKER got the peerless race mare YO TAMBIEN, YO EL REY, REY DEL SIERRAS and other stars of the turf.*

Another major California racing man was Elias Jackson "Lucky" Baldwin, who established the Rancho Santa Anita, near Los Angeles, on part of which is the present-day Santa Anita racetrack. Baldwin bred three winners of the American Derby at Chicago, then the country's richest race for three-year-olds. The last of these winners, conceived in 1890, was the horse REY EL SANTA ANITA (out of the mare ALAHO). Baldwin sent this mare more than 250 miles to the Piedra Blanca Stud to be bred to George Hearst's stallion *CHEVIOT, imported from Australia. (An asterisk preceding a horse's name indicates foreign birth.)

George Hearst paid jockey Anthony Hamilton the sum of $7000 a year for first call on his services, and Hamilton rode many winners for him. Like most of his contemporaries, Hearst employed many black jockeys. Hamilton came to Hearst from James Ben Ali Haggin and he also rode for August Belmont and James R. Keene appearing in every turf classic of importance in America during his heyday.

The largest Thoroughbred breeding operation ever known was located in California. James Ben Ali Haggin stood as many as thirty stallions and had 562 broodmares in foal, according to his catalogue of 1902, and his young stock totaled over two thousand head. Haggin and his law partner, Lloyd Tevis, owned 400,000 acres in Kern County, and a million more acres in New Mexico and Arizona.

The site of Senator Leland Stanford's Palo Alto horse farm is now Stanford University. Stanford will also live in equestrian history for proving that the running horse at full speed has all four feet off the ground at one point and that the weight of the horse is sustained entirely by each leg, one at a time, during the complete stride cycle. At his eleven-thousand-acre farm, Stanford commissioned a photographer named Eadweard Muybridge to set up a group of fast-shuttered cameras, the first of their kind, to create "motion pictures." The lens shutters were triggered by horses running down a camera-lined speedway, breaking control threads with their breasts as they ran. The entire series of horses, men, and other animals walking and running at different gaits, was published in 1887 as *Animal Locomotion*.

At San Simeon, meanwhile, George Hearst was planning, dealing, and spending to change his dreams of owning, breeding, and racing horses into reality. He had bought his first tract of land in 1865 for seventy cents an acre, and he planned to stable his broodmares and stand his stallions at stud there. He built a three-eighth-mile racetrack, sheds, barns, stables, and stalls for his horses—his heart's delight.

Fred Taral was a contract rider for James R. Keene but in 1889, on July 26, he won a purse riding MISS BELL wearing George Hearst's colors at Minneapolis.

Today, if you fly over San Simeon, the outline of the racetrack can be clearly seen from the air. Some of the stables and buildings are still used, and the track and broodmare barns are remembered by our friend, Pete Sebastian, the former postmaster, mayor, and owner of the general store in San Simeon. His father had been manager of Hearst's Thoroughbred horse operation.

During the winter of 1887–88, Hearst embarked on a major expansion of his racing and breeding activities. Although the Jockey Club, which regulates racing colors and other official matters, was not founded until 1894, Hearst did select his own racing colors—an orange-yellow shirt with green sleeves and an orange-yellow and green cap. Before, 1887, however, he often raced his horses in the colors of others.

In 1885, for example, John Mackey, James Ben Ali Haggin's stud manager, had selected for Hearst at the Rancho del Paso sale a bay yearling colt, KING FOX (KING BAN out of MAUD HAMPTON) for which he paid $710. Running in Haggin's colors, KING FOX turned out to be one of the best two-year-olds of 1886, winning the Saratoga and Kentucky Stakes at Saratoga and the Flatbush Stakes and Great Eastern Handicap at the Sheepshead Bay course of the Coney Island Jockey Club. Unfortunately, KING FOX died that autumn and never went to stud.

George Hearst's primary goal for years had been the founding of a Thoroughbred stud farm. After he was appointed a United States Senator in 1886 (he subsequently served a full term, taking his seat in 1887), he was pleased to spend a considerable part of each year in Wash-

Albert Cooper, originally a jockey, trained horses for Lucky Baldwin for eleven years and for other California owners, including Theodore Winters and J. B. Haggin. In July 1890 Hearst hired him to replace Matt Allen and Cooper responded by saddling the winners of sixteen stakes and handicap races from July 26 to November 1.

ington near major racing centers. He purchased horses to race and, at the same time, he bought stallions and broodmares to stock his stud farm. He depended on the advice of Haggin, Winters, and Stanford, even though the latter's interest was focused chiefly on trotters.

In the autumn of 1887, his racing friends advised Hearst to hire Matt Allen as a trainer. Allen had a fine eye for good horses, which were then, as now, difficult to purchase from their owners. Fortunately, Hearst had a full purse. Allen was quite a turf character. He was dubbed by the press the "Kid-Glove Trainer" for his fancy clothes, which were always worn with white kid gloves. He wore the gloves even to sponge out his horses' mouths. More important than his sartorial idiosyncrasies, however, was the fact that he was a superb trainer who watched every detail. After leaving Hearst, he saddled many a winner for Diamond Jim Brady.

Allen picked some good horses in Kentucky, including GLEN ECHO bred by The Honorable W. E. Simms, and BANBRIDGE bred by Major Thomas' Dixiana Stud, a brown colt by KING BAN and a grandson of the great mare DIXIE, after whom the Thomas stud farm was named. In 1871, the famous horse artist Edward Troye painted a portrait of DIXIE, and in May 1907 this and fourteen other Troye portraits from the Thomas estate were purchased by the New York Jockey Club where they can be seen today.

Matt Allen recommended buying from Leland Stanford's Palo Alto stud farm the imported horse *PETER, JR., a flashy, brown three-year-old, which George Hearst renamed *SAN SIMEON. Hearst also bought the colts PHILANDER and KENNETH and the filly QUESTION from Stanford, and he leased an imported black filly, *GORGO, by the stallion ISONOMY, because Stanford would not sell.

At Matt Allen's suggestion, Hearst persuaded Theodore Winters of Rancho del Rio to sell him the mare ROSETTA, who became a star of the track. Matt Allen also purchased from Winters SURINAM, a chestnut colt foaled in 1885, a royally bred colt by JOE HOOKER, out of ADA by REVENUE.

Allen insisted that the Hearst horses running in the East must start training before being shipped. At the spring San Francisco race meetings of 1888, SURINAM won for Hearst, beating the best horses of Hearst's friends Haggin and Stanford. On April 21, opening day at the Bay District track, SURINAM won the Tidal Stakes, the richest event on the card, at a mile and a quarter, and three days later he won the richest race of the meeting, the Pacific Derby, at a mile and a half. Hearst's two-year-old PHILANDER also placed second in the Gano Stakes, the most important juvenile race in California.

At last, Hearst's dreams were coming to vivid life. His horses were headed for the first-class eastern tracks—Coney Island, Brighton Beach, Brooklyn, Morris Park, and Jerome Park, as well as the ones we still know today, Saratoga in New York and Monmouth Park in New Jersey. Tracks in Chicago were also racing meccas for the California owners.

The trip across the continent in the late spring of 1888, in

unheated railroad cars, had been hard on the Hearst string. SURINAM did not regain his spring form until August 4, when he won a Free Handicap at Monmouth Park, his last win of the season. Another three-year-old, the black filly *GORGO, won a Free Handicap at Monmouth on July 5 and the Siren Stakes at the Coney Island Jockey Club's Sheepshead Bay course on September 4. The stable's only other win that year was by the three-year-old QUESTION, who won a nine-furlong sweepstakes at the Brooklyn Jockey Club's Gravesend course on September 25.

With fifteen horses in the barn and only three winners, this was a disappointing beginning at the eastern tracks. George Hearst was not discouraged, however. He decided to winter his race horses at Sheepshead Bay and increase their number by making additional purchases.

Earlier in 1888, he had bought the most expensive yearling ever sold. James Ben Ali Haggin had decided to breed yearlings for the market, and in 1888 he held his initial sale in the East, shipping seventy-five yearlings to the Jerome Park course north of New York City, where they were inspected by potential buyers and readied for the auction sale taking place at Madison Square Garden on June 25. The star of the sale was KING THOMAS, a bay colt foaled in 1887 by KING BAN out of MAUD HAMPTON by HUNTER'S LEXINGTON, and a full brother to the top racehorses BAN FOX (1883) and KING FOX (1884). All three were bred by James Ben Ali Haggin at his Rancho del Paso near Sacramento. The expensive yearling had been named KING THOMAS in honor of Major B. G. Thomas of Dixiana Stud in Kentucky, since Thomas had owned the yearling's dam before she was sold to James Haggin.

As noted above, George Hearst had purchased KING FOX as a yearling, but had run him in Haggin's colors during his brilliant career as a two-year-old. KING FOX had died in 1886 and BAN FOX in 1887, so that when KING THOMAS was to be sold at auction on June 25, 1888, Hearst saw it as his last opportunity to get a racehorse of this illustrious breeding who could also prove valuable as a sire. Hearst was willing to pay a new world's record, the highest price in history—$40,000 for a yearling—a price that stood for many years.

In the sales ring at Madison Square Garden, then located on 26th Street, Auctioneer William Easton wielded the gavel as he faced horse people from all over the country. An account from *The New York World* reads:

> ...at 1:20 the sale began with lively bidding for the half-sister to PONTIAC, but the bidding became slow until the prize of the sale, KING THOMAS, the brother of BAN FOX and KING FOX, was led into the ring.

In 1890, the jockey William Midgeley won many important races for George Hearst, including the great Eastern Handicap at Sheepshead Bay on TOURNAMENT.

The racehorses of Senator George Hearst spent the winters of 1888–89 and 1889–90 at the Coney Island Jockey Club's Sheepshead Bay course near New York City.

There was suppressed excitement when the auctioneer announced he had been authorized to open the bidding at $5,000; …like a flash it went to $15,000, which was Phil Dwyer's bid. As the crowd began to applaud, Mr. Easton stopped and appealed to the audience not to occasion excitement by applauding as it might frighten the colts, perhaps to injury; … Senator George Hearst and a party of friends had seated themselves behind the auctioneer on the 26th Street side of the Garden.

The bidding went on by the thousand between Senator Hearst and Mr. Appleby, until $30,000 was reached. Then there was a pause. Pent-up emotion seemed to be straining against the thongs of safety with which Mr. Easton had bound the crowd. Appleby stood pale and trembling, and when an advance of $500 came from the Hearst party, Dave Johnson moved up to his partner's side and exclaimed: "Go on, Luce, I'm with you!"

By the thousand the competitors went at it again, until the Senator's bid of $37,500 caused the crowd to rise and look anxious. Mr. Easton held his gavel off, while Appleby was the cynosure of all eyes. "Walk the colt around a little," said Appleby to the groom. A moment of intensity, then, "$38,000!" comes from Appleby. There is a stillness like death. The Senator nods his head negatively to the appeal of the auctioneer. As the gavel descends, a wave of applause overcomes judgment and breaks through the Garden. The colts in their stalls around the far walls become frightened and try to stampede, but the excitement is suppressed in time to avoid injury.

In the meantime, Mr. Appleby was surrounded by friends, who congratulated him on his pluck, and to questions as to his intentions regarding the colt he said would be trained next year and would win the Futurity, although it was admitted that sentiment and business went together in causing the phenomenal price to be paid for the colt.

The sale of KING THOMAS *for $38,000 completely eclipses the English record, although it has been said that an Englishman would pay a higher figure for a yearling than anyone else in the world.*

The newspaper went on to relate that on the following day, Senator Hearst offered Appleby and Johnson a $2,000-dollar profit for their colt, a total of $40,000 dollars. His offer was accepted and the horse was sent back to California to be developed and trained and added to the great breeding stud on the Senator's ranch. Hearst had had good luck with KING FOX, a full brother to KING THOMAS, but, sad to say, KING THOMAS, like many a high-priced yearling, was a disappointment. Instead of being given a few preliminary races against moderate opposition in which he could have established self-confidence, KING THOMAS first started in the top race for two-year-olds, the Futurity Stakes at Sheepshead Bay, in which he finished last. He never won a race; his best effort was as a three-year-old in the Bowling Brook Handicap, where he ran second.

Not all the Rancho del Paso yearlings of 1888 had been shipped east to the June 25th sale at Madison Square Garden. In fact, some of the choicest animals had stayed at home. In the autumn of that year, after the adjournment of Congress, Senator Hearst again sought the advice of John Mackey on Haggin's yearlings. They selected three by the New Zealand-bred stallion, *SIR MODRED: a filly named GLOAMING out of TWILIGHT by NORFOLK; a colt named TOURNAMENT out of PLAY-THING by ALARM; and a colt named BALLARAT out of FAVORITA by GLENELG. From Leland Stanford, Hearst bought RHONO, a chestnut colt, and, on the advice of Marcus Daly, a filly named MISS BELL.

The stable began its 1889 season with eleven two-year-olds to be added to the horses in the East. That year, Hearst had six winners. TOURNAMENT won the prestigious Great Eastern Handicap on September 12 at Sheepshead Bay and the Holly Handicap at Gravesend. His 1889 earnings totaled $14,517. BALLARAT won the Hudson Stakes at Gravesend on May 8, and placed several times for total earnings of $8,740. *GORGO won two races at the New York Jockey Club's Morris Park, the Record Stakes on October 5, and a Handicap Sweepstakes on October 9. Other winners were PHILANDER, MISS BELL, and BAGGAGE, in all a considerable improvement on the 1888 season.

The year 1890 was by far the best for Senator Hearst's racing stable. During that season, eight of his horses won twenty-four races.

One of these, TOURNAMENT, was the largest money earner of the year, and Hearst had the pleasure of being elected president of the Saratoga Racing Association. The change in his fortunes began in mid-July when Matt Allen was replaced as trainer. Although the horses had been wintered at Sheepshead Bay, they were far from fit when the season opened in May. While the stable's western division managed to pick up five races between April 9 and July 24, Matt Allen's charges could account for only two. GLOAMING won the Elms Stakes at Morris Park on June 5, and TOURNAMENT won the important Realization Stakes at Sheepshead Bay on July 2. *Turf, Field & Farm* reported:

> *There were nine starters for the Realization:* TOURNAMENT *and his stable companion* KING THOMAS; *the Belmont pair,* HER HIGHNESS *and* PADISHA; *the Western crack* PALISADE; TORSO, RANCOCAS, BANQUET *and* JERSEY PAT. *It was the most valuable race of the year so far, and certainly the poorest as a spectacle, for there was never but one in it, and that was* TOURNAMENT. *He was ridden according to Hayward's own idea, which was to go out and make the pace. This he did with a vengeance, for by the time the race was half over*

Tournament by Henry Stull. George Hearst purchased TOURNAMENT as a yearling in 1888 from his breeder James Ben Ali Haggin. In 1890 as a three-year-old TOURNAMENT, ridden by William Hayward, Sr., won seven stakes races and earned $89,535, which made him the leading money winner for that year.

William Hayward, Sr., started riding for George Hearst in 1889, winning a number of races, but his greatest triumphs were aboard TOURNAMENT during 1890.

TOURNAMENT had strung his field out for a furlong, and keeping on at a steady canter he won ultimately under a pull by fifteen lengths from HER HIGHNESS and BANQUET who made a close struggle for the place, their nearest attendant being PADISHA, who was fifteen lengths behind the pair.

Hayward rode TOURNAMENT in the Realization according to his own ideas and free from instruction and he had a "swell" [big] bet on his mount.

When Hearst replaced the dazzling dandy Matt Allen, he chose a black trainer, Albert Cooper, who had been born in Richmond, Virginia, in 1850. When slavery and the Civil War ended, Cooper was already an experienced horseman. As a child he had been a rider of race-horses, many of them notable winners, before he became a trainer. He worked his way to Chicago and the Washington Park Track there before moving on to California to "Lucky" Baldwin, where he spent eleven years producing winners. From Baldwin he went to train for Theodore Winters and then to J. B. Haggin. Because of Cooper's wide experience, Hearst was elated to hire him to be in charge of training. Hearst felt confident that under Cooper his horse TOURNAMENT would do well, and so he did.

Following his win in the Realization on July 2, Cooper entered TOURNAMENT in the Lorillard and Stockton Stakes at Monmouth Park, in

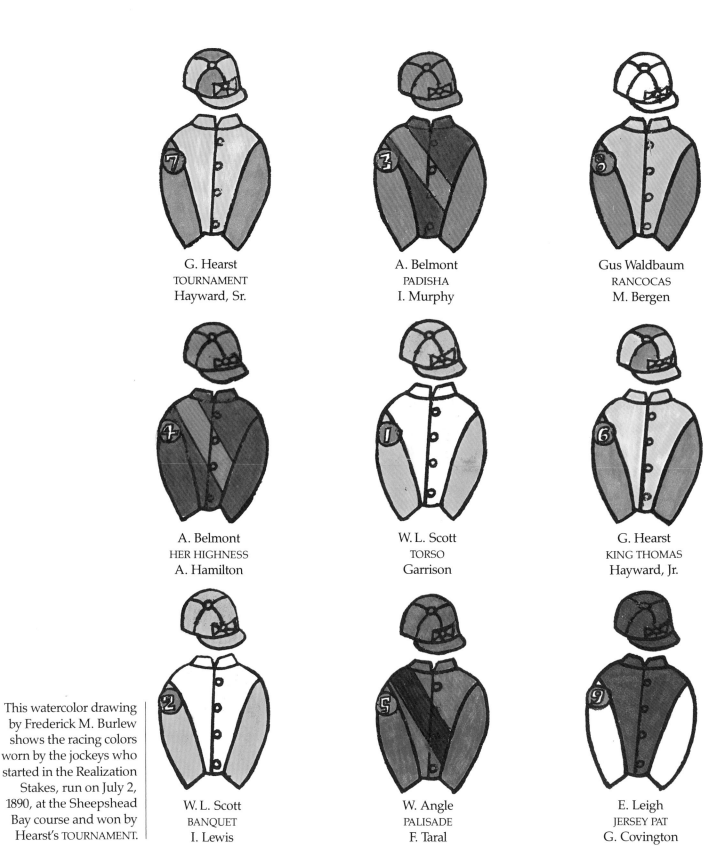

G. Hearst
TOURNAMENT
Hayward, Sr.

A. Belmont
PADISHA
I. Murphy

Gus Waldbaum
RANCOCAS
M. Bergen

A. Belmont
HER HIGHNESS
A. Hamilton

W. L. Scott
TORSO
Garrison

G. Hearst
KING THOMAS
Hayward, Jr.

This watercolor drawing by Frederick M. Burlew shows the racing colors worn by the jockeys who started in the Realization Stakes, run on July 2, 1890, at the Sheepshead Bay course and won by Hearst's TOURNAMENT.

W. L. Scott
BANQUET
I. Lewis

W. Angle
PALISADE
F. Taral

E. Leigh
JERSEY PAT
G. Covington

both of which the horse finished second. The new trainer then decided to freshen the entire stable and to get them fit. TOURNAMENT started again at Monmouth on August 19 where he won the Omnibus Stakes and $19,700. He then won six stakes in a row from August 23 to October 11, one at Monmouth, one at Sheepshead Bay, and four at Morris Park.

TOURNAMENT thus became the leading money earner of 1890, with a total of $89,535.

Cooper was also successful with other Hearst horses. From July 29 to September 28 the four-year-old RHONO won a Free Handicap and the Delaware Handicap at Monmouth, the Adirondack Handicap at Saratoga, and the Holly Handicap at Gravesend. The two-year-old YOSEMITE won a sweepstakes at Morris Park and three handicaps at Linden Park, New Jersey, while MISS BELL won a Free Handicap Sweepstakes at Monmouth.

In the November 1890 issue of *The Breeder & Sportsman*, Senator Hearst from the Golden State stood third on the list of winning owners with a total of $108,680. His winning horses, TOURNAMENT, YOSEMITE, BALLARAT, and others were entered in various races for the year 1891. But by February 28 of that year, their owner lay dying in his mammoth gray pile of a mansion at 1400 New Hampshire Avenue in Washington. His wife and son were holding his hands when he stopped breathing.

The nation's press mourned his death with his family. His colleagues in the Senate wrote and spoke with emotion:

> *Success such as that achieved by George Hearst is not a mere accident, nor the result of chance or luck. It can only be obtained by those qualities which were his ... industry, perseverance, good judgment and truth. During his life he was ever a hard and undaunted worker.... He was true to his work and his friends, and these were true to him. His nature was honest, rugged and kindly....*
>
> *He endured all the privations of the miner ... hard labor, coarse fare, fatiguing journeys over mountains and deserts ... for two fifths of a century.... I knew him in prosperity and in adversity. He was the same simple, genial, cheerful, delightful companion under all circumstances....*
>
> *He was a typical Californian, in ready risks and dash, in money making and money spending.... He held to his death an unabated love for his comrades of the olden times; ... he never found one of them in need that he did not supply his wants; ... they knew that George would replenish their empty pockets....*

The sporting magazines wrote of Senator Hearst's contributions to racing. Sanders D. Bruce, editor of *Turf, Field & Farm* (New York) in its March 7, 1891, issue wrote:

> *Not only racing men but the entire community heard the news with grief, for Senator Hearst was a fine type of the citizen of whom Americans have the greatest right to be proud, and, little as the turf could spare him, it was not only in racing circles that his death left a conspicuous gap. He has been a most prominent figure in Eastern racing circles, his colors of "green and orange" having been among the most popular seen on our race courses....*

The inaugural meeting at the magnificent Morris Park Course in Westchester County, New York, was held on August 20, 1889. That year Hearst's filly *GORGO won important races there on October 5 and October 9. In 1890, Hearst's horses were again successful at Morris Park, but the most impressive record is undoubtedly that of TOURNAMENT, who won four stakes races there on October 1, 3, 7, and 11, a feat that no horse would be asked to duplicate nowadays.

The Kentucky Livestock Record praised his sportsmanship, his popularity, the fact that he was a game loser and a modest winner, and went on to guess, "It is understood that William R. Hearst, the son of the dead turfman, will continue the racing stable."

In its lead article for March 7, 1891, *The New York Sportsman* said, "Few owners of racing stables, even among those whose names have been familiar from generation to generation, succeed in attaining so great a degree of popularity as did Senator Hearst.... The personality of the man was such that to know him was to like and respect him, and, comparative newcomer as he was, the victory of the green and orange was inevitably hailed with pleasure...."

Friends remembered examples of Senator Hearst's earthy wit, his honest simplicity. He seldom wore evening dress and would protest against going to the capital's gala entertainments, but he would sometimes succumb to Phoebe's persuasion with "Puss, if you want me to go, I'll go."

The old friends and the foods of the mining camps suited him. He dined on gold plates but preferred pork, spareribs, and hominy grits to terrapin. After a sumptuous luncheon, Mark Twain once complained to Mrs. Hearst: "I have been discriminated against, given filet of beef and lobster, while George was served hominy grits and greens with ham."

One of Senator and Mrs. Hearst's many protegés remembered that "the Hearsts were the biggest and best experience in the lives of everyone they met."

Phoebe worded it best on the bronze tablet installed on the

mining building of the University of California that she erected in her husband's memory:

> *...The stature and mold of his life bespoke the pioneers who gave their strength to riskful search in the hard places of the earth;... taking his wealth from the hills, he filched from no man's store and lessened no man's opportunity.*

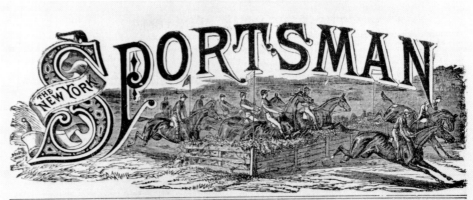

VOL. XXXII.—NO. 10824.
OFFICE, 45 MURRAY STREET.

NEW YORK, SATURDAY MARCH 7, 1891.

$4.00 PER YEAR IN ADVANCE,
SINGLE, COPY, TEN CENTS.

SENATOR GEO. HEARST.

BORN SEPT. 3, 1820 —DIED MARCH 28, 1891.

Few owners of racing stables, even among those whose names have been familiar from generation to generation, succeed in attaining so great a degree of popularity as did Senator Hearst, whose connection with the turf dates back but a few years. Expected as the news had been, the sorrow felt when it was learned that he passed away last Saturday night, was none the less deep and genuine. The personality of the man was such that to know him was to like and respect him, and comparatively newcomer as he was, the victory of the green and orange was inevitably hailed with pleasure. There was no more popular man, and this generally conceived opinion was singularly correct. He was the true type of American, approachable despite his wealth, bluff, off-hand, genial and sympathetic.

Senator Hearst was one who had carved his own way in the world through all the rough experiences and cruel vicissitudes that the West of old days could afford. He did not attain wealth in one bound, and it was not till after years of hard and patient toil that he accumulated the magnificent fortune from the abundance of which he was always so ready to help others. His native place was in Franklin county, Mo., where his father, a native of South Carolina, but of Scotch descent, had engaged in stock raising. Some twelve years after, graduating from the Franklin County Mining School in 1850, Senator Hearst left his native place to seek gold and fortune in California, and there after meeting with varying success he at length attained such prominences that he became engaged in politics. After running unsuccessfully for the Governorship of California in 1882, and receiving the Democratic vote in the State Legislature for the United States Senate in 1885, he was appointed United States Senator in March, 1886, in succession to Senator Miller who had died, and in January of the following year he was re-elected for the next term. At the time of his death Senator Hearst was not only the senior member of the firm of Hearst, Haggin & Tevis, and owner of most extensive and profitable mines in Arizona, California, Colorado, Mexico, Oregon and Idaho, but was one of the greatest real-estate owners in California. Until 1887 he was also proprietor of the San Francisco Examiner, but in that year he gave this property to his only son, Mr. William Hearst, who was born in 1863.

It was in 1881 that Senator Hearst first appeared prominently before the public as an owner of race-horses, though without a doubt before that period he had been interested in at least one race-horse of high quality, this being King Fox, the winner of the Saratoga Stakes, the Kentucky Stakes, the Flatbush Stakes and the Great Eastern Handicap. However, the son of imp King San and Maud Hampton never ran in his colors but under the name of Mr. Haggin, and hence it is more proper to date his debut from the beginning of 1888, when Gorgo, whose racing qualities he had leased from Senator Leland Stanford, Surinam, Question, Pillander and Merrimac, an Australian bred mare, ran in his colors. The string was a small one, but with Gorgo and Surinam, the success attained was quite flattering. Gorgo, the imported daughter of Isonomy and imp Flirt, by Hermit, was foaled in 1885, and consequently was a three-year-old in 1888. The previous season she had only sported silk once, that being when she had carried Senator Stanford's colors to victory in the Palo Alto Stakes at Sacramento. There are still many good judges of a racehorse who think that if ill-luck had not pursued her all through her active career, she not only would have proved a racemare of the very highest quality, but would have been a worthy rival for the 'Queen of the Turf,' Firenzi. During 1889 Gorgo ran six races, being first twice and second once. Her victories were in the Siren Stakes at Coney Island, which she won in a canter, with Yum Yum, Peg Woffington and

THE LATE SENATOR HEARST.

Her Ladyship, to all of whom she was conceding weight, behind her, and a handicap at Monmouth, at a mile, in which she beat Inverwick, George Oyster and six others. In the Bridge Handicap at Coney Island she ran second to Taragon, to whom she was conceding 5 lbs. actual weight, with Larchmont, Santalene, and Tristan behind her. If her jockey Littlefield had not bungled she should have won on this occasion also. Surinam scored brackets three times out of five starts. His first two victories were brought off at San Francisco, where he won the Tidal Stakes and the Pacific Derby. After coming East he ran third in the Harvest Handicap at Monmouth to Firenzi and Exile, and then after running unplaced in the Navesink Handicap, won a handicap at one and a quarter miles, in 2:09½, also at Monmouth. The other members of the string did not render any very good account of themselves, but the start made was encouraging enough, and it was not surprising that in 1889 Senator Hearst launched out on a more extensive scale.

big venture Ballarat had been secured at the Rancho del Paso sale for the sum of $5,000, while Tournament cost $3,500. It was then a valuable string of the greatest promise that went into Mat. Allen's hands, and the prospects were that the Senator's name would stand high on the list of winning owners.

That it did not do so was no doubt partially due to a most extraordinary and deplorable concatenation of misfortunes. Everything went wrong and ill-luck pursued the horses from the Spring onward in as marked a sequence as good fortune followed the colors of the Hon. W. L. Scott until the contrast between the two stables became a kind of proverb. During the Winter Tournament was so sick a colt that it was thought impossible for him to live, and indeed he did not get into anything like his true form till late in the season. Gorgo was in first-rate trim in the early part of the season, as she demonstrated by running third in Baceland's Suburban with 110 lbs. on her back, and indeed had not Hamilton been quite so anxious to set the pace with her, she might have

done better, and anyhow, would in all probability have wrested the place honors from Terra Cotta, who had all he could do to beat her. Just after the Suburban, however, she wrenched her shoulder at Sheepshead, at and not until the Fall meeting at Morris Park could she again face the flags. Then Ballarat, who started the year in great shape, winning the Hudson Stakes at the Brooklyn Spring meeting, and running second in the Great American and other stakes, went wrong at Monmouth and never regained his form.

King Thomas, as we all remember, proved a bitter disappointment, and besides exhibiting considerable temper, was found to have the bad mouth which has hitherto proved such an obstacle to his success, while Anaconda went lame at the beginning of the Monmouth meeting, and at the same place Gloaming injured her back and was never really fit again that season. And in addition to the bad luck of the horses themselves, the evil star of the stable seemed to be in the ascendant in other ways. Anaconda undoubtedly won the Double Event, yet the race was given to Torso, and the majority of those who saw the race were just as certain that Golden Horn beat Picnic in a race at Westchester. In the July Stakes Gloaming had her tail toward the winning post when the flag fell, and King Thomas was just as hopelessly left in the Great Eastern Handicap. In the Titan Stakes at Jerome, Tournament would have been returned victor in all human probability, but for a scrimmage at the start that knocked him nearly off his legs.

It would have been no surprise if the Senator had concluded that racing was not a sufficiently attractive pastime, but luckily he was not a man of that grain. He "faced the music" with all the pluck he had manifested when having "gone broke" in Sacramento he struck out on a fresh line in quest of fortune. The result as regards his racing in 1889 cannot be thought satisfactory. Still, although Ballarat did not regain his form Tournament won the Great Eastern Handicap at Sheepshead and the Holly Handicap at Gravesend in the Fall, while Gorgo won the Record Stakes at Morris Park and an overnight event.

At the beginning of last season the prospect of the "green and orange" assuming a very prominent position in the list of winning owners, seemed excellent. The three-year-olds appeared likely to be a particularly strong card, with Ballarat, who was thought to be the "king-pin" of the bunch, Tournament, Gloaming, Anaconda,

During 1888 sundry high-priced yearling had been purchased in order to obtain two-year-olds of the class requisite to form a foundation of a high-class racing stable. In the first place the racing world had stood aghast when after the great bookmaking firm of Appleby & Johnson had paid $38,000 for the last joint produce of imp King Ban and Maud Hampton, the Senator from the Pacific Slope took the youngster off their hands for the gigantic sum of $40,000. Why he should have done so is no doubt partially explained by the fact that King Fox though never sporting his colors was in reality running in his interests, and the idea was to get another of such superlative merit. Besides this

Miss Belle, Goldie, Horn, King Thomas, etc. while during 1889, the Senator had bought some choice yearlings, paying $10,000 for the sister to Dewdrop, and $5,000 for the half brother to Exile. That neither of these last have justified their claims to prominence is a matter of history. Fireworks never did better than run third, while hitherto the half brother to the quondam pride of Brighton Beach has never sported silk.

To tell the truth, the prospects of the stable began to look very blue indeed, after a month or so of the season had elapsed. Tournament had run eight races, and still had not earned brackets, while Ballarat had shown that he would not do at any dis-

Chapter 7/The Piedra Blanca Stud

A prince is never surrounded
By as much majesty on his throne
As he is on a beautiful horse.

—William Cavendish,
Duke of Newcastle

*I*n spite of his failing health, Senator Hearst's racing and breeding programs were still expanding in 1890 and early 1891. In
addition to the Piedra Blanca stud farm at San Simeon, he had established a second stud farm at Pleasanton. His two-year-olds were being
trained at the San José course, and for the reception of his racehorses the
following autumn he was also constructing a training center at Suñol.

In those days the death of an owner automatically cancelled
the future racing engagements of all his horses. To guard against this
and because of his illness, Senator Hearst transferred the ownership of
his horses to a partnership that included his only child, William
Randolph Hearst.

George Hearst died in February of 1891 and by the terms of his
will the entire estate was left to his widow, Phoebe Apperson Hearst.
Since she didn't wish to continue racing, she decided to sell the horses in
training. The mares, however, continued to be bred to the Piedra Blanca
stallions in 1891, 1892, and 1893, and sixty-nine foals were born there in
1891 and 1892. George Hearst died only two years after the arrival of his
first major crop of foals. In consequence he did not live to enjoy the
success as a Thoroughbred owner and breeder that was rightfully his.

The records of the Piedra Blanca Stud have not survived,
although there exist published accounts of Hearst horses sold after his
death at public auction. From these, and volumes four through seven of
the American Stud Book, it has been possible to reconstruct an adequate
picture of the Piedra Blanca breeding operations.

When George Hearst began buying the various tracts that
eventually became the San Simeon ranch, his goal was the founding of a
stud farm, which he called Piedra Blanca after the promontory on the
property where the earliest lighthouse in California once stood. Through
his trainer Matt Allen, he purchased a number of horses to race and at

Theodore Winters (1823–1894) was California's first major Thoroughbred breeder, the fortunate owner of two highly successful stallions, NORFOLK and JOE HOOKER. George Hearst relied on Winters' advice and purchased five of his broodmares, four by NORFOLK and one by JOE HOOKER.

the same time he bought stallions and broodmares to stock his Piedra Blanca Stud Farm, relying largely on the advice of his friends James Ben Ali Haggin, Theodore Winters, and Leland Stanford.

The first foal recorded in the stud book was dropped in 1883. From 1883 to 1888, a total of twelve foals are credited to Hearst as a breeder. His big years, when he personally planned the matings of his stallions and mares, were 1889, 1890, and 1891. During this period, seventy foals were bred by Hearst at San Simeon. From 1883 to 1893, a grand total of 151 foals were born at San Simeon, certainly qualifying it as a major breeding operation.

These foals were the produce of forty mares. Twenty-four had been purchased from American breeders, six were mares imported from Australia, and ten had been bred at Piedra Blanca. Of the twenty-four, seven were purchased from James Ben Ali Haggin, four more from Theodore Winters, two from Leland Stanford, and three from other Californians (A. J. Hutchinson, Dan N. Burns of San Francisco, and an unknown California breeder supplied one each), making twenty-nine California-bred mares in all.

Commenting on Hearst's career in the United States Senate, Joseph Cairn Simpson, editor and publisher of the San Francisco weekly *Breeder and Sportsman,* later wrote, "He is for California first, last and all the time, a hearty advocate of her interests, and a willing champion of her cause." Certainly this viewpoint was reflected in Senator Hearst's choices of broodmares.

In selecting stallions to put to his broodmares, George Hearst went further afield than California. One of the most influential students of bloodstock breeding of the time, was the Australian-born C. Bruce Lowe. His book, *Breeding Racehorses by the Figure System,* published posthumously in 1892, established the taproot tail female lines (mothers, mothers, mothers) which are still included in present-day Thoroughbred auction sales catalogues. Bruce Lowe convinced Hearst's friend Haggin that Australian bloodlines would make a valuable addition to American Thoroughbred breeding. In 1886, Haggin imported to his Rancho del Paso the New Zealand-bred stallion *SIR MODRED who had had a brilliant racing career in Australia. The horse fulfilled his expectations as a most successful stallion.

Two years later, on behalf of Senator Hearst, Haggin bought *SIR MODRED's brother *CHEVIOT, two years younger but already a proven racehorse. Foaled in 1879 by TRADUCER out of IDALIA by CAMBUSCAN, the bay horse had been bred by the Middle Park Stud Company of New Zealand. In Australia he had won the Canterbury Derby, the Midsummer Handicap (2 miles, 120 pounds), and the Craven Stakes (1¼ miles, 133 pounds). Only *SIR MODRED was able to beat him for the Canterbury Cup.

From New Zealand early in 1888, *CHEVIOT arrived at Piedra Blanca, where he was given a full book of mares. In 1889, Hearst bred nine foals by *CHEVIOT and purchased two more, while in 1890 he bred eleven by his imported stallion. In 1891, however, only four foals by *CHEVIOT were bred by Hearst at Piedra Blanca.

The 1892 crop of two-year-olds by *CHEVIOT and bred by Hearst also compiled an impressive racing record. CASTANET, a chestnut filly out of CARRIE C., won at four and a half furlongs; MEZZOTINT, a chestnut filly out of DAISY S., won at five furlongs; ADOLPH, a bay colt out

George Hearst's Ranch House by Paul McNamara

of MERCEDES, won at San Francisco; PRIZE, a bay filly out of SISTER TO LOTTERY, won a race with fifteen starters in Washington Park, Chicago; and BRIDAL VEIL, a chestnut filly out of NELLIE COLLIER, won the Ladies' stakes at St. Paul, Minnesota. PRINCESS, another two-year-old by *CHEVIOT, bred by Leland Stanford out of MUSIC, won at half a mile.

For the dispersal sale of the Hearst horses-in-training the world's foremost auction firm, Tattersalls of London, was chosen to stage-manage what the newspapers called "one of the greatest sales of Thoroughbreds ever held."

At this sale of his horses in New York, three of the two-year-old colts by *CHEVIOT sold exceptionally well—VERNON for $7,500, OSRIC for $6,600, and GONZALEZ for $6,100. All three were purchased by the partnership of Walcott and Campbell of New York. OSRIC won the

San Simeon is a treasure trove of work by architect Julia Morgan. This seldom-seen warehouse was designed to resemble a mission in the town of San Simeon.

In 1864 Theodore Winters bought NORFOLK, an unbeaten stallion sired by the great LEXINGTON, for $15,001, one dollar more than the price of his sire. The arrival of NORFOLK at the Yolo County stud farm signaled the rise of California as a major Thoroughbred breeding center.

Expectation Stakes at Sheepshead Bay on the following day, while GONZALEZ won one race in 1891 and four in 1892. The May 23rd issue of *The Spirit of the Times* said: "The high prices realized for the get of *CHEVIOT was a triumph for the Australian blood. That the get of an untried sire should reach such figures was rather unexpected."

The sale was held at the Sheepshead Bay course on May 14, 1891. The sales ring was pitched in the open, and the auctioneer was stationed under a spreading apple tree. All the celebrated racing figures of the day gathered: L. O. Appleby, who had bid against Hearst in the past for the record high-priced yearling, KING THOMAS; Joseph Clark; Senator P. H. McCarron; Fred Gebhardt, H. J. Jerome; the Dwyer brothers. Their faces, well known in the racing world, had greedy gleams in the eyes. Young Foxhall Keene, a leading gentleman rider and son of James R. Keene, had a determined set to his jaw.

The May 23rd issue of *The New York Sportsman* described the sale as follows:

> It was some few moments from 12 o'clock when Auctioneer Easton
> silenced the clatter about the Brooklyn Handicap, and the possibili-

ties of picking the winner, by announcing from the rostrum that the sale was about to begin. He paid a deserved tribute to the memory of the late Senator Hearst, and it may be remarked here that the death of that estimable gentleman was a great misfortune to the turf, for the showing made by his horses at the Brooklyn meeting was such as to convince even the most pessimistic that his would have been one of the strongest, if not the very strongest, stables on the turf this year.

There was a ripple of applause as TOURNAMENT, *the winner of $89,000 last year, was led into the arena. As fit as a fiddle, as hard*

James Ben Ali Haggin (1821–1914) founded the Rancho del Paso near Sacramento in 1885 and it soon became the largest Thoroughbred stud farm in history. Haggin was the breeder of TOURNAMENT, George Hearst's most successful racehorse, and the source of seven of Hearst's broodmares.

as nails, as handsome as a picture, and as sound as a bell. That's what TOURNAMENT *was as he stood there under the apple tree, his satin jacket shining as though he had been oiled.*

"Here we have a horse, one that you all know," was TOURNA-MENT'S *introduction, and Fred Gebhardt, who had sat listlessly looking at the catalogue he held in his gloved hand, took in the big colt at a glance. He whispered to his friend Howland Robbins, who sat by him, and Mr. Robbins nodded assent. When Mr. Easton called for a bid a pale-faced young man with a dark moustache took a position behind the auctioneer and almost beneath a well-executed*

Senator Leland Stanford (1824–1893) established his Palo Alto Stud in 1876 to breed both Thorough-bred runners and a large number of trotters. In 1872 he financed the photographic experi-ments of Eadweard Muybridge, who pro-duced the definitive work on the gaits of the horse.

Elias Jackson (Lucky) Baldwin (1828–1909) founded his Rancho Santa Anita Stud near Los Angeles in 1876. In 1890 he sent his mare ALAHO to the Piedra Blanca Stud to be bred to *CHEVIOT, and she produced REY EL SANTA ANITA, winner of the 1894 American Derby in Chicago, then the country's richest race for three-year-olds. The present Santa Anita racetrack is located on part of what was the Baldwin ranch.

portrait of TOURNAMENT *that hung suspended from the limb of the tree. It was Foxhall Keene, one of our crack gentleman riders, and son of James R. Keene....*

The bidding was fierce, see-sawing back and forth with Foxhall Keene always toppling the other contenders, until it was evident that the competition was at an end for $33,500. The newspaper reported that "there was considerable applause when the colt was knocked down

IMPORTED CHEVIOT

WINNER OF THE CANTERBURY DERBY, MIDSUMMER HANDICAP AND
CRAVEN STAKES, AUSTRALIA.

*Is in the Fairview Stud of Messrs. Charles Reed & Sons, Gallatin, Tenn.
Yearlings sold annually.*

CHEVIOT, bay horse, brother to Sir Modred, foaled 1879, bred in the Middle Park
Stud, New Zealand, by Traducer, dam Idalia by Cambuscan, grandam Dulcibella
by Voltigeur, out of Priestess by The Doctor. Imported Sir Modred and Cheviot
were both great race-horses in Australia, and both have become decided successes
in the stud in America. Cheviot won the Canterbury Derby, Midsummer Handicap,
2 miles, 120 lbs., and Craven Stakes, 1¼ miles, 133 lbs., and only Sir Modred, his
brother, could beat him for the Canterbury Cup. Cheviot is still at the beginning
of his stud career. With the same opportunities, he will take equal rank with his
older brother as a sire. Among his get, very limited in number, are the following:
Osric (winner of the Expectation Stakes last year), Gonzales (a winner last season
and of four races this year), Dr. Ross, Vernon, Bernardo (who has captured five races
this year, 6 furlongs in 1.15, 1.15¼ and 1.16¾, each time with 119 lbs., 7 furlongs in
1.26, with 124 lbs., and 1 mile 70 yards in 1.48), Princess, half a mile in 0.48¼, with
115 lbs.), Castanet (4½ furlongs in 0.58⅖), Mezzotint (a two-year old winner this
year at 5 furlongs), Adolph (another two-year old, that defeated a good field this
spring at San Francisco), Prize (a two-year old winner at Washington Park, Chicago,
this year from a field of fifteen), and Bridal Veil (winner of Ladies' Stakes, St.
Paul, Minn., this year). Cheviot's sire, Traducer, was bred in England, by The Libel
(son of Pantaloon) and Arethusa. Traducer was the best stallion that ever stood in
New Zealand. From 1867 to 1881 he got nine winners of the Canterbury Derby, the
greatest event in that country, viz.: Scandal, Envy, Defamation, Calumny, Trump
Card, Natator, Sir Modred, The Dauphin and Cheviot. In three of these years his
get ran first, second and third, and in two others first and second. He also got Van-
guard (winner of the New Zealand Cup), Welcome Jack (winner of the Canterbury
Cup), and Lurline, a great mare, out of imp. Mermaid. Lurline produced Darebin,
who won the Victoria Derby of 1881, and the best horse of his time throughout Australia. Traducer was to New Zealand and Australia what Lexington or Leamington was
to us, or Hermit was to England. Idalia, dam of Cheviot and Sir Modred, was the only
Cambuscan mare imported to the colonies. She produced Betrayer, Sir Modred,
Idalium, Cheviot, July, all by Traducer, Liverpool by King of Clubs, chestnut filly
by Apremont, and a bay filly by Apremont. Betrayer won the Canterbury Champagne Stakes, Canterbury Cup, Wauganal Cup and Timaru Cup. Sir Modred won
the Dunedin Champagne Stakes, Canterbury Champagne Stakes, Dunedin Cup, Canterbury Derby, Timaru Cup, Dunedin Birthday Handicap, Canterbury Cup, Christ
Church Plate and the Sydney Great Metropolitan. July ran second for the Dunedin
Cup. Liverpool won the Welcome Stakes. Cheviot won the Canterbury Derby,
Midsummer Handicap and Craven Stakes, and only Sir Modred, his brother, was
able to beat him for the Canterbury Cup. Idalia was the Pocahontas of New Zealand, the queen of its stud. In blood she is rare, being a sister to Onslow (who beat
Cremorne, in England, in 1871) by Cambuscan, out of Dulcibella, who won the Ce-
sarewitch in 1860. Thus her grandams are old Bee's-wing (Newminster's dam), South-
down (Alarm's dam), and Martha Lynn (Voltigeur's dam.) Cheviot should be a grand
stallion. (See Sir Modred, page 254.)

This is an advertisement published in 1892 for the New Zealand-bred stallion *CHEVIOT, purchased in 1888 for George Hearst by James Ben Ali Haggin. The twenty-four foals sired by *CHEVIOT between 1889 and 1891 by Hearst compiled a successful racing record.

130

and the name of the purchaser announced. The young man purchased TOURNAMENT for himself, and it is understood that Albert Cooper will train for him, while William Hayward will be the jockey."

The twenty-six horses brought a total of $128,100. As for "the portrait of TOURNAMENT that hung suspended from the limb of the tree" with his jockey William Hayward up, this was by the accomplished equestrian artist Henry Stull, and it is reproduced in this volume.

The yearlings foaled in 1890 were sold in 1891 as one lot to Mr. Dan ("White Hat") McCarty of California, while in 1893 more yearlings were taken to New York by Mr. J. G. Follansbee and sold together at auction. These included EULALIE, a chestnut filly by JIM BROWN out of *FUN, and a bay colt by JIM BROWN out of *BEAUTY.

At still another sale on July 18, 1893, the Piedra Blanca yearlings were sold at auction by Killip and Company at San Francisco Salesyard at the corner of Van Ness Avenue and Market Street. The printed catalogue listed nineteen lots with one added, the twenty horses averaging $520 apiece with a few bringing $1,000 or more.

The final dispersal of the Piedra Blanca Thoroughbreds was held November 20, 1893, an auction sale conducted by the same firm at the same place. It included stallions SURINAM ($3,600), fifteen-year-old JIM BROWN ($500), *TRADE WIND ($145), *SAN SIMEON ($300), TRUE BRITON ($100), *DR. ROSS ($190), and *DEL MAR ($1,000).

Thirty-six mares were sold, of which one third brought $1,000 or more apiece. Three of them had been purchased from Theodore Winters, including SISTER TO LOTTERY, by MONDAY, dam of the winners PROXIMATE, LORENA, and PRIZE ($1,300), NELLIE COLLIER by JOE HOOKER, dam of YOSEMITE, VERNON, and BRIDAL VEIL ($1,075); and PROXIMATE, a five-year-old by NORFOLK out of SISTER TO LOTTERY ($1,000). EVERGLADE, purchased from J. B. Haggin, a six-year-old mare by IROQUOIS, American-bred winner of the Epsom Derby (England), brought $2,700, while the English-bred *FUN purchased from Leland Stanford brought $2,600. Another California mare was MISTLETOE ($1,100) by THAD STEVENS, bred by J. B. Chase and purchased from Dan Burns of San Francisco. Mares purchased by Hearst in the East included VIOLA by HIMYAR, dam of MELODY, bred at the Dixiana Farm, Lexington, Kentucky ($1,400); DECEPTION by TEN BROECK, a seven-year-old bred by C. D. Farrar of South Carolina ($1,400), and MISS PICKWICK by *MR. PICKWICK, a five-year-old mare bred by Charles Reed of the Fairview Stud, Gallatin, Tennessee ($1,100), which had earlier purchased the Piedra Blanca stallion *CHEVIOT. Highest-priced of the American mares was COSETTE, bred by George Hearst at Piedra Blanca in 1887; she sold for $5,000. Her sire was the famous JOE HOOKER out of ABBEY purchased from Theodore Winters, and she was a half sister to OSRIC, a bay colt bred by Hearst. Completing the dozen mares sold were two imported from Australia: *GERTRUDE, who had been a fine race mare there ($1,600), and *PALOMA,

THE HORSEMAN

An Illustrated Journal, Devoted to the Interests of the Horse, his Owner and his Friends.

VOL. XIV.—NO. 26.   CHICAGO AND NEW YORK, THURSDAY, JUNE 28, 1894.   SUBSCRIPTION $4.00 PER YEAR.
SINGLE COPIES 10 CENTS.

REY EL SANTA ANITA BY IMP. CHEVIOT—ALAHO, BY GRINSTEAD.

Rey El Santa Anita by
George Ford Morris

the sale topper ($7,500), a high price fully justified by the racing exploits
of her offspring.

The chestnut mare *PALOMA is an excellent example of the
success of the Piedra Blanca breeding by F. Reynolds in Australia and

At the dispersal sale of Senator Hearst's horses-in-training, held on May 14, 1891, at the Sheepshead Bay course, Foxhall Keene, an internationally known polo player and a Master of Foxhounds, became the new owner of the great racehorse TOURNAMENT, securing him with a final bid of $33,500.

imported by Hearst. For Hearst and for the Hearst estate, she produced three colts and two fillies from 1890 to 1894, one by JIM BROWN and four by SURINAM. *PALOMA was purchased for $7,500 by Burns and Waterhouse of San Francisco. In his chapter devoted to the Burns and Waterhouse partnership, Thomas B. Merry, author of *The American Thoroughbred* (1905), wrote:

> *PALOMA, an Australian-bred mare was purchased from the estate of the late Senator Hearst. Among her produce we may mention YELLOW TAIL by WATERCRESS, the best three-year-old of 1900; ARMITAGE by SURINAM, a stake winner both in California and at the East; PALOMACITA, a good winner in California; MISS ROWENA, a winner of $11,255 in three seasons, winning five consecutive races at two years and six at three, making a total of 26 wins in all; DON CLARENCIO, a repeated winner, and EXAMINER, a winner at the East.

Other particulars as to the success of the Hearst Thoroughbred breeding program are set forth in the sections dealing with the Piedra Blanca stallions, with *CHEVIOT in this chapter, and with other stallions in the appendix.

CATALOGUE

OF

Thoroughbred Yearlings

AND THE RACE HORSES

KING THOMAS

AND ALMONT

FROM

SAN SIMEON RANCHO

PROPERTY OF THE ESTATE OF THE LATE

George Hearst

AT AUCTION AT SALESYARD, COR. VAN NESS

AVE. AND MARKET STREET

AT 11 A.M.

Wednesday, July 19, 1893

KILLIP & CO.

LIVE STOCK AUCTIONEERS   22 MONTGOMERY STREET

CATALOGUE

OF

THOROUGHBREDS!

Stallions and Broodmares,

ALSO,

Trotting-Bred Stallions and Broodmares,

FROM THE

SAN SIMEON RANCHOS,

PROPERTY OF

Estate of Hon. GEO. HEARST,

AT

PUBLIC AUCTION,

AT 11 A. M. ON

Monday, November 20, 1893,

AT

Salesyard, Cor. Van Ness Ave. and Market Street,

KILLIP & CO., Auctioneers,

22 MONTGOMERY STREET,   SAN FRANCISCO, CAL.

The November 20, 1893, catalogue of the final dispersal sale of Piedra Blanca breeding stock concludes with a section entitled "Trotting Horses." The preface to the catalogue said merely, "Of the trotting stock we will say that, almost without exception, the horses offered are well-bred, and from families of known worth."

The catalogue lists twenty-seven mares and two stallions. Five mares, all of them by ECHO, 462, owned by Californian L. H. Titus, were foaled in 1882. Three of these were "Standard," that is, had trotted a mile in two minutes, thirty seconds or less. Four of their daughters (two of them Standard) and one son are also listed. There are four other mares by ECHO, only one (1883) with a foaling date. Three mares, two of them Standard and all foaled in 1883, are daughters of ALASK by ELECTIONEER, 125, the great Palo Alto son of Rysdyk's HAMBLETONIAN owned by Leland Stanford, one of history's greatest breeders of trotting horses.

The number-one Piedra Blanca stallion offered was INDIRECT, a brown stallion foaled in 1885, by DIRECTOR, one of the most influential sires in Standardbred pedigrees, the property of Monroe Salisbury of California. The dam of INDIRECT, also offered for sale, was DIXIE, a bay mare foaled in 1882 by ECHO, 462. INDIRECT was thus a three-quarter brother in blood to DIRECT, also foaled in 1885, who in 1892 set the world's pacing record of two minutes, five-and-a-half seconds. He had previously campaigned as a trotter, winning four out of six starts in 1888 and six out of eight in 1889. DIRECT became one of the most important sires

in the Standardbred registry; he was the great-great-grandsire of the extraordinary pacer and sire BILLY DIRECT. In purchasing trotters as well as Thoroughbreds, George Hearst selected horses bred in California.

Perhaps it was the influence of Leland Stanford, then also a United States Senator, which persuaded George Hearst to acquire trotting stock. At any rate the sentence in the preface to the catalogue noting that "the horses offered are well-bred and from families of known worth" is a masterpiece of understatement.

Hearst did not live to savor his triumphs either as a breeder either of trotting horses or Thoroughbreds. Because of his death in February 1891, only two years after the arrival of his mares' first foals, these foals were sold as two-year-olds at a public auction in New York. The yearlings bred in 1892 by his estate were sold in San Francisco, and the remaining stallions, broodmares, and young stock were also auctioned there.

It was the purchasers at these sales who reaped the benefits of the Hearst breeding program, for George Hearst was, in fact, one of the most successful early California breeders of Thoroughbreds, a success for which he did not receive credit.

He piled up the gold for his heir and his widow, yet nothing in his long, arduous, adventurous life—no riches, no honors, no pleasures—gave him more satisfaction and more enjoyment than his winning Thoroughbred racehorses.

George Hearst's hard-earned gold had helped him realize his dream of owning a famous racing stable and a Thoroughbred breeding farm at San Simeon. He held onto that dream—dear to his heart—until his tough old heart stopped beating.

Part III/ The Golden Heir, William Randolph Hearst

Chapter 8/The Morgans and Morabs

Morgan!—She ain't nothing else,
and I've got the papers to prove it.
Sired by Chippewa Chief, and twelve
hundred dollars won't buy her.
Briggs of Turlumne owned her. Did
you know Briggs of Turlumne?—
Busted hisself in White Pine and blew
out his brains down in Frisco?

—Bret Harte

illiam Randolph Hearst, George's only son, began to buy and breed Morgan horses when he inherited from his mother, Phoebe, a golden horde of wealth that included not only the San Simeon ranch, but also a ranch in Mexico of a million acres, one thousand square miles of land in Vera Cruz and Yucatan, plus many thousands of acres of timber forest on one of the few rivers that flows all year long in California near Mount Shasta. And that was only a part of the fortune in gold mines and other assets.

He began at once to build his hilltop castle and to indulge his taste for art, antiques, and good horses. He continued the largesse shown in 1900 by his munificent mother, who had given money for an archaeological exploration around the mission San Antonio de Padua, which had owned most of the Hearst land. After sixty years of neglect following its secularization, the once prosperous and proud mission was now in ruins. Hearst gave $50,000 toward the restoration of the mission and later set up a fund of half a million dollars for all of the California missions. He also enlarged his inheritance by purchasing other Mexican land grants, so that at one time the Hearst ranch extended to 250,000 acres. Not until he faced financial disaster did he sell this land, reducing his holdings to what his parents had left him. No matter what tales are told about how his long-time friend, Marion Davies, gave him the money, it was the sale of this land that saved his empire.

But back to the horses! While W. R. Hearst inherited his taste for art, antiques, and history from his mother, his love of horses and land certainly came from his father. Although he did not fox hunt, play polo, or compete in trail rides or shows, he rode well and could spend

hours in the saddle. He wanted to be well mounted and he must have decided that the Morgan was the best breed for him, the one that was truly, wholly American. Although my friend, the Quarter-Horse historian Alexander MacKay-Smith, and others might claim otherwise, Hearst believed the Morgan was the first true breed developed in America.

Several other breeds of horses are of American origin, such as the Quarter Horse, the Narragansett Pacer, the Tennessee Walking Horse, the Missouri Fox Trotter, the American Saddle Horse, and the Standardbred.

Look at the years some of the United States registries were founded:

1873–Thoroughbred
1891–American Saddle Horse
1894–Morgan
1908–Arabian
1935–Tennessee Walking Horse
1936–Palomino
1938–Appaloosa
1940–American Quarter Horse
1958–Missouri Fox Trotting Horse
1976–Hearst Memorial Morab

Although the use of horses for all kinds of farming, including cattle raising, has declined, the recreation-horse population of the United States has zoomed up. All breeds except ponies (because children are riding larger horses) have expanded, according to the Department of Agriculture, and the most popular breeds in America are Quarter Horse, Thoroughbred, Appaloosa, Tennessee Walking Horse, American Saddle Horse, and Arabian, in that order.

Of the world's major breeds the Morgan is unique in that all registered Morgans descend in the male line from a single sire, JUSTIN MORGAN, who was foaled about 1789. Yet no one can be absolutely sure of the lineage of the Morgan horse for there is no documentation about the parentage of that first Morgan. The horse may have been sired by a Thoroughbred stallion named TRUE BRITON, an English hunter owned by the De Lancey family of Westchester County, New York. The De Lanceys may have bred him themselves or imported him; in any event, Colonel James De Lancey, one-time commander of the British Army's Westchester Light Horse Troop, rode the horse with pride and then lost him to American soldiers who captured the steed and spirited him off to White Plains, which was a territory held by the Americans.

A frequent San Simeon guest from Hollywood was Arthur Lake, who usually played Dagwood, the comic-strip character, in the movies. Here he plays a cowboy with a Morgan horse.

Not until after the Revolution was the stallion TRUE BRITON brought out of hiding. He was advertised in 1788 as standing at stud at the stable of John Morgan in West Springfield, Massachusetts. His name had been changed to BEAUTIFUL BAY. John Morgan, it seems, was a cousin of Justin Morgan, a sometime singing teacher, sometime horse breeder. Justin Morgan is said to have bred a mare to his cousin John's horse. The mare produced a bay colt that Justin Morgan named FIGURE. Others say he took the bay colt from his cousin John to settle a debt. Anyway, the bay colt, FIGURE, is said to have carried a pedigree in his dam's line back to the GODOLPHIN ARABIAN. Indeed, Arabians have been mentioned in the background of both the sire and dam of Justin Morgan's stallion.

From West Springfield, Massachusetts, the singing teacher Justin moved his family to the rugged country area of Randolph, Vermont, where he advertised in local newspapers in 1793 and 1795 the stud services of his stallion FIGURE. The severe cold and the harsh life of rocky Vermont put Mr. Morgan into an early grave, but the bold, gentle stallion that he had bred and trained survived him for many years.

From farm work to racing to covering mares, the beautiful bay stallion became known by the name of his breeder, JUSTIN MORGAN, and performed gallantly until 1821. It was his three sons that established the Morgan traits of speed, style, and stamina. They were SHERMAN, BULRUSH and WOODBURY, and from them all registered Morgans descend.

RED DOT, one of Hearst's fine Morgan broodmares

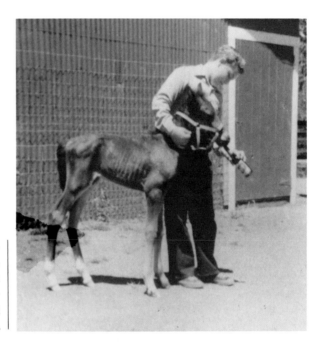

W. R. Hearst's grandson, twelve-year-old John, nicknamed Bunky, often helped around the stables. Here he feeds an orphaned Morgan foal.

The Morgan is small by comparison to the Thoroughbred, maturing to 15.2 hands, although some individuals are smaller and some taller. The ideal stallion and mare somewhat resemble powerful, heavy Arabians. Breeders strive for high action, a small refined muzzle, large eyes, small ears, a slightly dished or straight (never Roman) nose, a smoothly crested strong neck, a long croup with very little slope, and a high tail carriage. Morgans look rounded of contour and short coupled, with an upright head carriage caused by extremely sloping shoulders. Overall substance in neck, quarters, and barrel with a refined head—that is "the Morgan look."

By 1850, descendants of JUSTIN MORGAN had become the most popular horses in the United States, even with American presidents. Benjamin Harrison drove a roadster behind a team chosen by his Secretary of War, Mr. Proctor, a native of Vermont. Franklin Pierce was trotted around the capital by a pair of Morgans, and Abraham Lincoln, on becoming president, purchased a matched pair of Morgans for $3,000 from upstate New York. Confederate generals, including Robert E. Lee, fought Yankees from the backs of Morgans.

General Thomas Jonathan "Stonewall" Jackson's Morgan horse, LITTLE SORREL, had been captured for the General's use at Harper's Ferry, and he was riding the celebrated Morgan when he was killed. Douglas Southall Freeman, the Civil War historian, described the horse: "His skill in letting down drawbars was amazing. In the same

way he could take the rails off a fence until it was low enough for him to jump."

A Morgan horse traveled to California with the gold rush in 1849. His name was ST. CLAIR and he walked ahead of a team of oxen. In California, he sired a great many trotting horses and when the Morgan registry was formed, he was given the number 48. Among the millionaires who could afford the best were many Morgan owners, such as William Ralston and James Ben Ali Haggin. While neither they nor other early settlers kept careful pedigrees, the California ranchers upgraded their horses by breeding them to handsome Morgans.

In the West during the late nineteenth century and the early twentieth, one man became the largest breeder of the old-fashioned Morgan bloodlines: Mr. Richard Sellman of Mountain Vale Ranch in Texas. He bought a stallion descended from JUSTIN MORGAN's son BULRUSH and helped to preserve the original Morgan traits. Mr. Sellman, in turn, interested a Mr. Roland C. Hill of California in raising Morgans. It is said that Mr. Hill traveled to Texas to choose his horses and hired a railroad boxcar to haul his purchases back to his ranch, the Horseshoe Cattle Company, in California. He purchased a young stallion, PAT ALLEN, from J. C. Brunk, another early breeder, back in Rochester, Illinois. PAT ALLEN and another stallion, QUERIDO both crossed magnificently with the mares that Mr. Hill had purchased from Sellman. It was from Mr. Hill that William Randolph Hearst got his first Morgans.

The most ancient and valuable Morgan blood shows up in the pedigrees of the Hearst horses. For example, GENERAL GATES was the foundation Morgan stallion chosen as sire for the U. S. Government Morgan Horse Farm, established in Vermont in 1906 to breed and supply the American cavalry with mounts. Even as early as the Civil War, the U. S. War Department had decided that the Morgan horse, with his easy gaits, soundness, courage, and good sense, would make the ideal breed for cavalry horses.

GENERAL GATES, a great-great-grandson of BLACK HAWK, has had an important genetic influence on present-day Morgans, the true American warmbloods. In 1930, Hearst purchased a grandson of GENERAL GATES. He was UHLAN, a bay stallion, bred by the U. S. Morgan Horse Farm. UHLAN's dam was POINSETTIA, who was in turn sired by TROUBADOUR OF WILLOWMOOR, who showed in his pedigree seventy-one crosses to the original JUSTIN MORGAN.

In 1929, Hearst had purchased his first fourteen Morgan mares from Roland C. Hill. Twelve of these mares were sired by an excellent young stallion, PONGEE MORGAN, bred by J. C. Brunk in Illinois. The other two were sired by QUERIDO, a great-grandson of GENERAL GATES. The dams of all fourteen mares were from the Sellman group. Most of them being sired by RED OAK, a son of GENERAL GATES. The stallion UHLAN was bred to the Hearst mares for the 1931 and 1932 seasons.

BLOSSOM'S LASS |

Hearst then sent this magnificent stallion temporarily to his ranch in Mexico to upgrade the horses there. The well-known Quarter Horse mare SUPRESO traces her pedigree back to UHLAN's stay in Mexico.

Hearst bought eight more mares from Roland C. Hill in June of 1931. All eight were daughters of GENERAL GATES' grandson, QUERIDO; all were out of mares of the old Sellman stock. For his Morgan breeding program, two more stallions were purchased by Hearst: MOUNTCREST SELLMAN in April 1932 and HACIENDA CHIEF in March 1940. Both of these

The historic Morgan sire GENERAL GATES was a great grandsire of this Hearst-bred mare, PIEDMONT ALVA, foaled in 1932. Her pedigree shows many other Morgan greats, including MAJOR GORDON, BABE, and BLACK BESS.

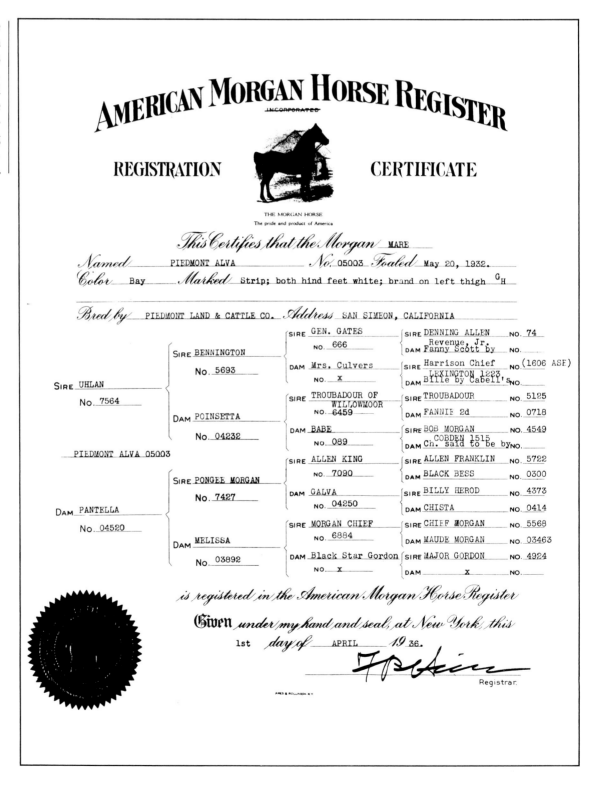

AMERICAN MORGAN HORSE REGISTER
INCORPORATED

REGISTRATION   CERTIFICATE

THE MORGAN HORSE
The pride and product of America

This Certifies that the Morgan   MARE

Named   VIOLET RAY   *No.* 04573 *Foaled* April 1928

Color Bay   *Marked* Blackpoints; Brand "88" on thighs.

Bred by ROLAND G. HILL   *Address* KEENE CALIFORNIA

				SIRE GENERAL GATES		SIRE DENNING ALLEN	NO. 74
		SIRE BENNINGTON		NO. 666		DAM FANNY SCOTT	NO. --
		No. 5693		DAM MRS. CULVERS		SIRE ---	NO.
SIRE QUERIDO				NO. ---		DAM ---	NO.
No. 7370				SIRE ETHAN ALLEN 3d		SIRE ETHAN ALLEN 2d	NO. 406
		DAM ARTEMISIA		NO. 3987		DAM BAY by GREEN MOUNTAIN	NO. 493
		No. 02731		DAM CH. M.		SIRE BOB MORGAN	NO. 4549
VIOLET RAY 04573				NO. ---		DAM CH.M.by MORGAN TIGER	NO. 816
				SIRE GENERAL GATES		SIRE DENNING ALLEN	NO. 74
		SIRE RED OAK		NO. 666		DAM FANNY SCOTT	NO. --
		No. 5249		DAM MARGUERITE		SIRE WHITE RIVER MORGAN	NO. 482
DAM REDOLSY				NO. 01635		DAM BAY	NO. --
No. 04813				SIRE THE ADMIRAL		SIRE JUBILEE DE JARNETTE	NO. 3854
		DAM RED DAISY		NO. 4871		DAM BROWN	NO. --
		No. X04210		DAM ---		SIRE ---	NO.
				NO. ---		DAM ---	NO.

is registered in the American Morgan Horse Register

Given under my hand and seal, at New York, this

31st *day of* December 19 28.

Colgate Mann

Registrar.

Hearst's purchase from Richard Sellman of the stallion MOUNTCREST SELLMAN produced the mare PIEDMONT EVELINA.

stallions were grandsons of another famous sire, HEADLIGHT MORGAN, out of Sellman-bred mares.

If you examine the old registration papers of those early Hearst Morgans, such as PIEDMONT SELLMAN (foaled in 1933 by MOUNTCREST SELLMAN out of BUTTERFLY), you will find that they all carried the blood of illustrious horses, not only GENERAL GATES, but also ETHAN ALLEN, MAJOR GORDON, and others who descended from the original JUSTIN MORGAN.

From 1932 through 1939, 110 Morgan foals were registered by the San Simeon Stables. Among them were eighteen Morgan-Arab crosses who were permitted in the Morgan register. (In those days a certain degree of outside blood was permitted.) They were identified as "Morabs" by an *X* placed in front of their registration numbers. These Morabs were born to registered Morgan mares and were sired by the Arabian stallions GULASTRA, RAHAS, SABAB, ANSARLAH, GHAZI, JOON, and KASAR. Only one colt in this group was an exception. He was ANTMAN

Roland Hill another early California breeder, sold the mare VIOLET RAY to W. R. Hearst; foaled in 1928, this mare shows GENERAL GATES several times in her pedigree.

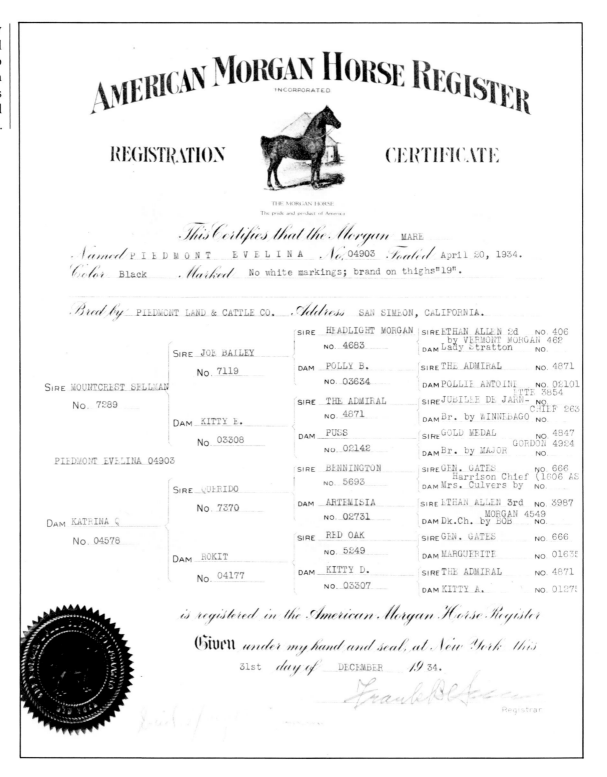

150

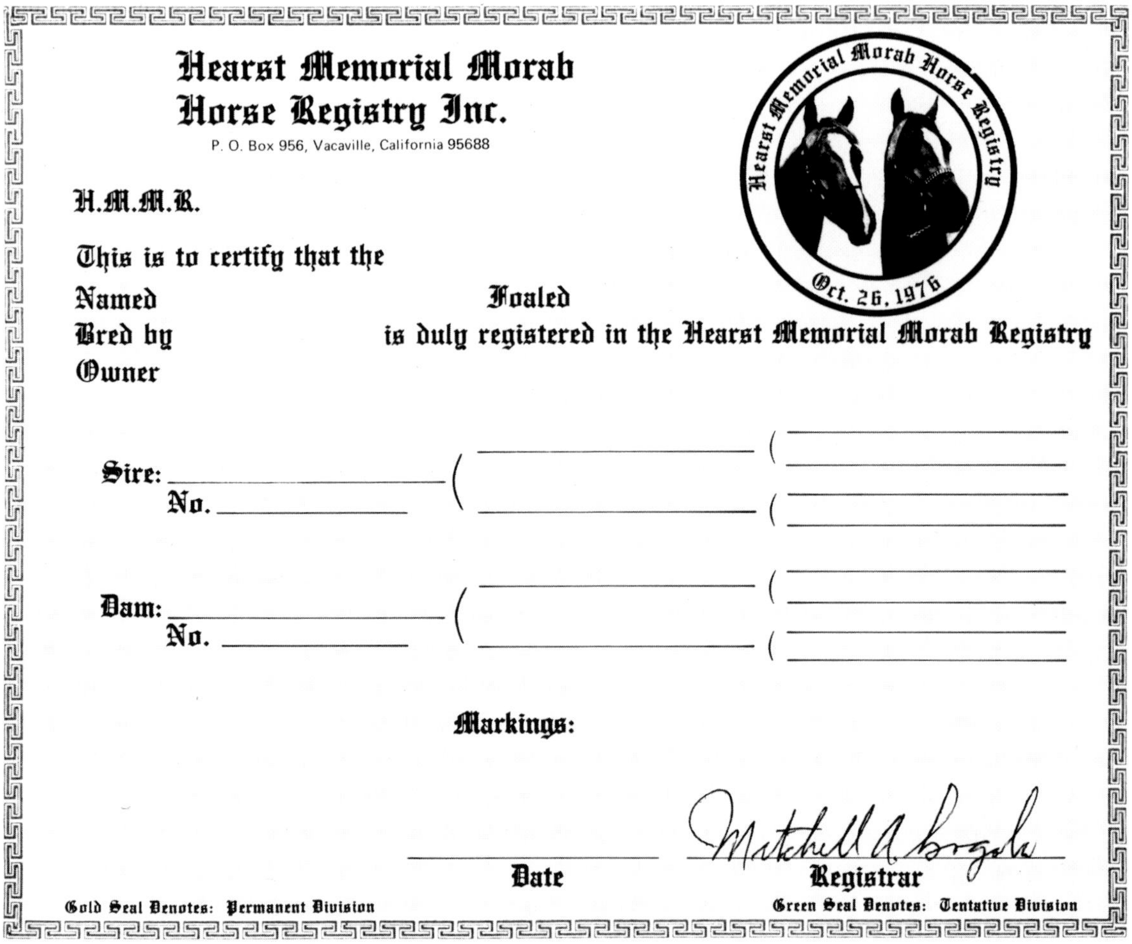

Hearst Memorial Morab Horse Registry Inc.

P. O. Box 956, Vacaville, California 95688

Hearst Memorial Morab Horse Registry
Oct. 26, 1976

H.M.M.R.

This is to certify that the

Named   Foaled

Bred by   is duly registered in the Hearst Memorial Morab Registry

Owner

Sire: ____________

No. ____________

Dam: ____________

No. ____________

Markings:

____________ Date

Registrar

Gold Seal Denotes: Permanent Division

Green Seal Denotes: Tentative Division

This is one of the registrations for the Hearst Memorial Morab Horse Registry, Inc.

X8318 and he had been sired by the Morgan MOUNTCREST SELLMAN. His dam, PONTEZ, was half Arabian, sired by the Arabian stallion ANTEZ out of a PONGEE MORGAN daughter.

After buying the Morgans and Arabians, nothing could have been more natural for Hearst than the idea of crossing these two fine breeds and starting a new one. The Morab breed now has a registry of its own, founded in 1976. Spearheaded by John and Patricia Florence Marsh and other interested breeders, it is known as the Hearst Memorial Morab Registry in honor of William Randolph Hearst. Mrs. Marsh, an adventurous horsewoman, confirmed for me that some of W. R. Hearst's Morabs had been sent to Mexico where he planned to improve the inferior horses there.

There are several other Morab horse organizations. One of them, the North American Morab Horse Association, in Wisconsin, publishes an excellent magazine called *Morab World* for all owners of Morab horses. They point out that a Morab should be a blending of characteristics of the Morgan and the Arabian. They also give credit to William Randolph Hearst for originating the name "Morab."

Old California newspaper clippings describing the foundation

of the Hearst Memorial Morab Registry described the ideal as follows:

> ... *a fine head, the ears are small, alert with a slight inward curve. The Morab has a straight slightly dished profile, large dark eyes set wide apart, large nostrils, is broad of cheek and has a narrow muzzle. The neck is thick and set on a fully sloped shoulder; short in back, hips long, broad in the chest.*

Between 1932 and 1947, there are several gaps in the records of Morgan offspring registered by the San Simeon ranch. Perhaps many of the mares purchased from Hill were sent to the ranch in Mexico where accurate records were not kept. In any event, twenty Morgans were sold at San Simeon at an auction held on September 2 and 3, 1947, a sale that included the famous stallions UHLAN and MOUNTCREST SELLMAN. On September 10, 1949, the last sale of any Hearst-owned Morgans was recorded.

A book could be filled with the names of prize-winning Morgans who are descended from the two foundation sires UHLAN and

MOUNTCREST SELLMAN. Four sons of UHLAN alone—PIEDMONT APACHE, KATRILAN, UHLAN-RO, and ENOWEE—sired champions without number.

Although Hearst's involvement with breeding Morgans was of limited duration, it greatly influenced the Morgan horse in the West. One group of breeders still produces quality Morgans that possess both disposition and conformation. These breeders are carefully preserving what they call the "Sellman-Hill-Hearst" bloodlines.

VIKING MYSTIC, another winning Morgan

BLOSSOM'S LASS |
The Phillip Morrisons' Aranaway Morgans started a dynasty in the Pacific Northwest with SONOMA, a grandson of UHLAN. From another UHLAN son, KATRILAN, are descended a number of champion broodmares, winners at both halter and performance.

In Missouri, James O. West and Marlene Peterson of Heritage Morgans have also made a large contribution to continuing the Sellman-Hill-Hearst Morgans. The foundation stock of these and other breeders originated in the grassy pastures of San Simeon.

The blood of the stallion UHLAN was also perpetuated by J. Clark and Effie Bromiley in central California. They owned UHLAN's grandson, TRILSON, who sired two famous Morgans, MUSCLEMAN and DAPPER DAN. For most of his life, DAPPER DAN headed the breeding program of Mr. and Mrs. Walter Kellstrom of Modesto, California.

ENOWEE, another son of UHLAN, sired a string of top showring mares in southern California. ENOWEE was out of a MOUNTCREST SELLMAN mare. A group of MOUNTCREST SELLMAN daughters were purchased by Mary Smith of Camarillo, California, who bred a fine band of black Morgans. Mary Smith's Morgans, which are identified by the prefix "Hedlites," have furnished several breeding farms with foundation Morgans.

MOUNTCREST SELLMAN also sired another colt, REDMAN, and his son BLACKMAN gained renown as a sire of first-class broodmares. Another son of MOUNTCREST SELLMAN was foaled in 1936 and sold to

VIKING CORONADO

O. C. Foster in Los Angeles. That son was MONTABELL, and Morgans of that line became identified with the suffix "Gift," such as the stallion SENATOR GIFT who was twice winner of California's Feather River Endurance Ride, a demanding test.

The UHLAN line has also been continued by Mrs. LaVonne Houlton at the Viking Morgan Ranch in Modesto, California. Mrs. Houlton had daughters of MUSCLEMAN as foundation mares and she has bred and shown many champions. I am deeply indebted to her for much of my information on the Hearst Morgans. A fount of Morgan history, Mrs. Houlton writes this tribute:

> *It is unlikely that William Randolph Hearst ever dreamed what an impact his relatively small breeding program would have on the history of the Morgan horse in the West.*

JAYE P. COLLINS |

Chapter 9/The Appaloosas

Light-footed streak of lightning
It was high spirited
I whipped up this flying steed
And was able to lay down my armor.

—Anonymous Chinese poet,
637 A.D.

Appaloosas at San Simeon by Sam Savitt. The mare in the foreground has a traditional Appaloosa "blanket"; her foal has a "snowflake" pattern, while the horse at the left rear is a "leopard" Appaloosa.

*W*R. Hearst owned a magnificent Appaloosa stallion, APPY. He was, I remember, one of my husband's favorite mounts and was later sold to a Hollywood movie star. The ranch at San Simeon often sold homebred Appaloosas to Hollywood movie cowboys, so Hearst horses appeared in countless Westerns for many years. However, no amount of digging and research has revealed registrations or the history of any of these Hearst Appaloosa horses. They were bred for good looks and pure pleasure, and in the early days breeders did not consider registrations to be important.

While film heroes favored these flashy horses as mounts, eons earlier, men of the Ice Age who followed the herds of animals into the middle of France hunted horses for food. These hunters, the Cro-Magnon men of fifty thousand years ago, drew pictures, including many spotted horses, in the caves where they took shelter. In these caves, created by ice melting and flowing streams of water, the hunters built fires, roasted their kills, and decorated the walls. Their discarded dinner bones reveal to modern archaeologists that wild horses, including the spotted ones, provided much of the hunters' food.

For generations these Stone Age people painted the smooth walls of the caves with oil and colored earth. They drew horses, wild oxen, reindeer, bison. These murals, protected underground, remain today as fresh, as vivid, as when they were painted, perhaps around 18,000 B.C.

Only later, around 5,000 B.C., did men learn to trap, to tame, to domesticate these wild sheep, goats, cattle, and wild horses. First horses were used for meat and only later for transport, around 3,500 years ago. Once he learned to ride, early man could roam widely on his swift horse, and tremendous value was placed on the horse. In Egypt as early as 1400 B.C., in fact, horses with spots were pictured accompanying their

The labels on the photo read: MRS. G. BARHAM, BILL HART, MRS. W.R. HEARST, GUY PRICE

Nine-year-old William Randolph Hearst, Jr., was all smiles with his friend cowboy star William S. Hart. The two Bills hit it off, and Hart was happy to have one of the San Simeon Appaloosas to ride as his movie horse.

owners into the afterlife. Spotted horses also appeared in Greece, decorating vases at about the same time. In ancient Chinese culture as well, spotted horses can be seen among early ceramic "tomb horses" and on murals and scroll paintings. The six war horses of Emperor T'ai Tsung, who died in the seventh century, decorated his tomb. Each horse, one of them spotted, was honored with a poem; the verse dedicated to the spotted horse opens this chapter. In early cultures then, of Egypt, Greece, China, Persia, and India, down through the ages, horses with spots were rated as treasured, uncommon mounts. In India, as late as 1949 when Prime Minister Nehru went to the opening of the Indian legislature, he ceremoniously rode a leopard-spotted horse.

Because the Hapsburg Empire in 1560 included both Spain and Austria, it was natural that Spain should provide her best horses as gifts to the Austrian court. The Hapsburg ruler of Spain, Philip II, sent to his uncle, the Emperor of Austria, his finest horses, which carried Arabian blood from the Moorish conquest of Spain. The horses with the most talent were used for breeding at the royal stud at Lipizza near Trieste, and their offspring were sent to the Austrian capital to join the school of equitation, now known as the Spanish Riding

School of Vienna and still considered the best in the world.

In 1727, Austria's court painter, Scottish-born Johann George Hamilton, painted the horses at the Emperor's stud farm at Lipizza. Surprisingly enough, typical Appaloosas seem to be prancing among the many other horses. In Austria a spotted horse was called a Pinzgauer; in fact, each country seems to have had a name for the horse we know as Appaloosa:

> Tigre—Argentina and France
> Heavenly Horse—China
> Knabstrubber—Denmark
> Chubarry or Blagdon—England
> Chubarri or Atigrado—Spain
> Kuran Dagh—India
> Guinduri or Wynduri—Mexico

APPY, a favorite mount of W.R. Hearst, Jr.

While horses with allover spots can be registered as Appaloosas, the preferred coloration is a dark horse with a white blanket over the rump sprinkled with dark spots. Vertical stripes running the length of all four hooves, a fairly short tail, a circle of white around the iris of the eye, and a mottled muzzle are other Appaloosa characteristics. Noted for his strong, tough legs, his versatility and endurance, the Appaloosa stands about 15 hands tall and weighs from 950 to 1,200 pounds. He has agility, speed, and a good disposition as well as being showy in appearance.

The Spanish sent to the New World shipments of horses, many of them spotted, soon after Columbus had crossed the Atlantic. For twenty-five centuries, the horse had served man for transport, conquest, and agriculture, and now he would help to develop the New World. Throughout the lands of the West Indies, Mexico, and Peru, the Andalusian horses would flourish with their masters. In 1519, Hernano Cortès brought with him a herd of sixteen horses, including "a dark roan with patches, and a Pinto with white stockings on his four feet," according to a contemporary chronicle.

In outlining this book, I knew that mere words could never tell the story as effectively as a few pictures. Some of the pictures, however, can only be imagined. Such as how the American Indians must have stared in astonishment when they saw horses for the first time. Scholars believe that one of the reasons so few Spanish could conquer Mexico so easily, capture the capital, and bring down the entire Aztec empire can be attributed to horses. As one Spanish conquerer put it: "After God, we owe the victory to the horse."

Legend persists that Indians first got horses because some Spanish horses had escaped to the wild, and their offspring were said to have spread and multiplied. Scientists and historians, however, question whether these horses could have survived cold, disease, predators, and accidents to populate the plains and provide Indians with the thousands of horses they eventually captured, tamed, and rode. Now it is believed that the Indians learned the care and culture of horses by taking care of Spanish mission livestock. The Spanish colonists used the Indians as stable help, to water, to feed, to clean and clean up after the horses, although they forbade the Indians to ride them. In spite of these prohibitions, however, the Indians did learn to ride, and it was only a matter of time before they began to steal the best horses. Later, the spanish traded horses with the Southwest Indians, and Indians brought food and other articles from far distances to exchange for the Spanish animals. By the end of the seventeenth century, the Navahos, Comanches, and Apaches were stealing horses in vast numbers from Spanish settlements.

Tribes near the Spanish colonies became the first Indian horse owners, but gradually horses spread to tribes in the North, East, and West. Soon the Navaho, the Crow, the Commanche, Shoshone, and the Blackfeet all became horsemen.

PLUCKEY'S TERCERO willingly clears a cross-country fence with Kim Reed in the saddle, showing the remarkable versatility of this handsome breed.

According to legend, the Nez Percé tribes of the Northwest (named "nose pierced" by the French because of their nose-piercing ceremonies) obtained horses around 1710 from the Shoshone. As soon as they were mounted, the Nez Percé learned to hunt buffalo like the Plains Indians, for it was much easier than fishing and hunting on foot. They became first-class horse breeders, castrating inferior stallions and selling or trading second-rate animals. Horses with spotted white rumps looked flashy up close, yet were camouflaged at a distance, ideal for war or buffalo hunting. Before long half of the tribes' horses were thus colored. By 1806 their spotted horses were renowned.

In that year the Lewis and Clark Expedition brought white men into Nez Percé country. Merriwether Lewis, an expert Virginia horseman, commented on the fine horses when his party ventured to the Nez Percé pasture lands. Next came the Hudson's Bay Company's white men and the trappers of Mr. Astor's company. Gradually the Indians traded and sold their celebrated horses, and they learned the way of the white men—to read and to write. In 1831, missionary families began to settle the Indians' country and soon came more and more white people.

White homesteaders by 1870 were farming in what is now Oregon, Washington, and northern Idaho and were calling the stream that ran through their country the Palouse River, a word perhaps derived from the Indian word *perlous*, which translates as "something sticking up out of the water." (Indeed, a giant ledge of rock does stick up in the river.) However, a French-Canadian word *pelouse* or *palouse* means "river with a green bottom," and that may be the true origin of the name.

In any case, the Nez Percé Indians specialized in breeding fine spotted horses along the river, and after a time the white homesteaders began to refer to an Indian horse with spots as a "Palousey." Perhaps some traveler mistook the homesteaders' word and called the horse an "Apalousey." The accepted spelling today is Appaloosa.

As more settlers moved into the Northwest the Nez Percé Indians and their magnificent horses were doomed. They lost their pasture land to broken treaties; they were forced to fight losing battles, to be hunted with their families, and, at last, to surrender.

Their chief, Joseph, made this moving speech when he surrendered to the Americans:

> *Tell General Howard I know his heart. What he told me before, I have in my heart. I am tired of fighting. Our chiefs are killed. ... It is cold and we have no blankets. The little children are freezing to death. My people, some of them, have run away to the hills and have no blankets, no food; no one knows where they are—perhaps freezing to death. I want to have time to look for my children and see how many I can find. Maybe I shall find them among the dead. Hear me, my chiefs. I am tired; my heart is sick and sad. From where the sun now stands I will fight no more forever.*

Their captured horses, numbering more than a thousand splendid animals, were sold at auction in 1877 by the United States. Hardy as they were, the Appaloosas were now dispersed and nearly

◄ Tim Katona and
Appaloosa BRAVO B
perform a sliding stop,
a requirement in this
junior reining class at the
National Appaloosa
Horse Show.

disappeared as a breed. But they did manage to survive.

Occasionally a Wild West show would have an Appaloosa. William P. Cody, known as Buffalo Bill, was immortalized by Rosa Bonheur, the French animal painter, riding a spotted horse.

Fifty years after the Nez Percé surrender and the auction of their animals, the Appaloosa Club was founded in 1938, with Claude Thompson as the first president. After some lean years, the club was granted recognition by the National Association of Stallion Registration Boards.

Portrait of a Piebald Horse from the Eisgrub Stud by Johann Georg von Hamilton. This handsome stallion of Italo-Hispanic origin was one of the stars of the Eisgrub Stud, where horses were raised to serve the Princes of Liechtenstein.

Today 233 regional clubs are growing and the registration of Appaloosa horses is over 450 thousand and increasing. Great Britain, Australia, Canada, and even Italy have clubs. The Amon Carter Museum of Western Art organized an exhibition and published in 1963 a book authored by the historian of the Appaloosa Horse Club, Dr. Francis Haines, who traces the ancestry of this ancient, unique breed. Certainly, of the many breeds that have pranced in the parade of Hearst horses, none has contributed more exotic color and dash to the fabled stables of San Simeon than these tough, hardy and outstanding spotted horses.

The Imperial Riding School in Vienna by Johann Georg von Hamilton. In this painting, Archduke Charles, son of the Holy Roman Emperor and destined to become King of Spain, is performing a piaffe with his Spanish stallion. Horses for the Imperial Riding School were bred in a variety of colors. Here we see a remarkably Appaloosa-like spotted horse and even a Palomino. It was not until the middle of the nineteenth century that pure white stallions became fashionable.

Chapter 10/The Palominos

When I bestride him I soar,
I am a hawk; he trots the air;
the earth sings when he touches it.

—William Shakespeare

*M*ost of us picture California as a golden state with golden hills, golden beaches, golden sun. Which horse fits into this picture? It can only be the golden horse—the shining, precious Palomino. These horses seem to be as shrouded in mists of myths as the unicorns. In all my research I could find no positive information about the origin of horses of that color or even of the name Palomino. Some say the Spanish name *"Ysabellas"* for golden horses derives from the Pope's colors, which were white and yellow. Since Queen Isabella was a supporter of the Pope, horses of a yellow color with white manes and tails became known as *"Isabellas"* or *"Ysabellas."* Others say that the Queen, who lived from 1451 to 1504, is known to have favored these dazzling horses, and that is the reason they are called *"Ysabellas."* Columbus, under the sponsorship of Spain, was the first to bring horses to the new world, so perhaps the word "Palomino" came from some early golden-colored horses that sailed with Columbus. Still others have claimed that the word *Palomino,* a well-known last name in Spain came down from some early colonists who bred horses of that color. In Spanish, "Palomino" also means a dirty, yellow shirttail stained with urine, a vulgar thought to say the least, and, we hope, irrelevant to the history of this decorative breed of horses.

Pick whichever theory pleases your fancy. All we know for sure is that the word *Palomino* referring to horses first appeared in print in California around 1920, and that golden horses existed in Europe and China hundreds of years before that. In the National Gallery of Art in Washington, D.C., you can admire a Palomino horse painted around 1482, ten years before America was discovered. In Botticelli's *Adoration of the Magi,* one of the seven horses is clearly a golden Palomino with a white mane.

In the chapter on Appaloosas I mentioned a painting by Johann George Hamilton that hangs in the Spanish Riding School in

W. R. H. and Don Pancho by Sam Savitt. Francisco (Pancho) Estrada inherited the Rancho Santa Rosa from his father and at the age of seventeen sold it to George Hearst, for whom he worked as a horseman. He stayed with the family for over sixty years.

The name of this dazzling horse is GALAGOLDEN GLOW, who is recorded in both the Palomino and Half-Arabian registries. He is the favorite mount of William Randolph Hearst, Jr. On the pommel of the saddle is another family favorite, Stonewall Jackson II, a Jack Russell terrier.

The Palomino stallion HARVESTER sired many early California Palominos. This photograph was taken at San Simeon.

Vienna. The painting, done in 1727, shows the broodmares at the imperial stud farm in Lipizza, and a mare of golden color with white mane and tail appears with the others. In Hamilton's painting of Archduke Charles on horseback, reproduced on page 167, one of the stallions is clearly a Palomino. In an earlier painting of the mid-seventeenth century, Queen Anne of England, wife of James I, is shown riding what appears to be a Palomino horse.

The Palomino DON PEDRO as he appeared in the advertisement for the Hearst reduction sale

In the early days of California, neither the Spanish, the Mexicans, the Indians, nor the Americans kept breeding records. Although they all admired the golden horses and propagated them, they kept no written pedigrees. Two early breeders in Texas, W. B. Mitchell and Berry Ketchum, produced creamy, golden horses, and in Colorado, Coke T. Robards stood at stud a celebrated Palomino stallion named OLD FRED. In Oregon, Ben Swaggart began as early as 1890 to breed horses of a golden color with flaxen manes and tails; he named them "Creamoline" horses. Sad to say, although the Swaggart horses attracted other breeders and cowboy stars such as Hoot Gibson, none of the breeding records was preserved after the deaths of Mr. and Mrs. Swaggart. Today the Creamoline strain of Palominos is carried on by Gene Beksinski, who has bred them since 1935.

A San José banker, Louis Oneal, made an important contribution to Palomino breeding, as did Dwight Murphy of Santa Barbara who had obtained his foundation stock from the horses bred by W. B. Mitchell in Texas. Other California strains were known as the "Lugo horses" and the "Dutra horses," presumably after the names of the men who bred them. The first documented Palomino horses seem to have come from a family ranch not far from San Simeon, south of Monterey. The Moreno or Montejo family had for generations bred and inbred golden horses with white tails and manes. Around 1915, a lady named Mrs. H. I. Farman of Sierra Madre obtained a stallion she named REY EL MONDO, and with that stallion she began to breed and show the golden horses seriously.

W. R. Hearst was a Californian and saw these golden horses as a California specialty and a novelty to boot. He loved the rare and the best of everything but as much as anything he loved horses. They were a natural for a big spender, a golden heir, and so he began to buy and breed Palominos with a passion.

In going through his old files searching for names and registration papers, Robert Dallmeyer, treasurer and secretary of the Palomino Horse Association, discovered that Hearst's chief stallion, DON PEDRO, had been foaled on April 15, 1937. DON PEDRO, who stood at stud at San Simeon, was often advertised in 1942 as "The Outstanding Palomino Stallion In The West." This stallion, who had so much influence on early California Palominos, was bred by Warren Shoemaker and later owned by Dwight Murphy of Santa Barbara, mentioned above. DON PEDRO appears as grandsire of many horses bred by Chester W. Scott of Lancaster of California, another early Palomino breeder.

DON PEDRO was foaled only one year after the Palomino registry was incorporated in 1936, but research on behalf of the Palomino Horse Association had begun early in the 1930s by enthusiast Dick Halliday. Hearst was therefore among the first to climb on the Palomino bandwagon. According to the records of the association, many of the

DON PEDRO

files were kept under the name of the ranch rather than of the owner and this was true of the Hearst horses bred at San Simeon.

Another sire of many Palomino champions, THE HARVESTER, was stabled at San Simeon; he himself was sired by CREAM OF WHEAT out of a Morab mare, RED DAWN. The Palomino HARVEST TRIGGER owned by movie cowboy Roy Rogers had the Hearst bloodlines and starred in many movies with his owner. (An entire movie was devoted to NAUTICAL, the Palomino show jumper, but he was not, as far as I know, related to any of these early Palomino horses.) Another organization, the Palomino Horse Breeders of America, also provided me with registration papers of Hearst horses, which indicate also that Hearst, like today's breeders, cherished the golden horse, the only breed with uniform coloring. Hearst also tried crosses with Arabians, Morgans, Morabs, and Quarter Horses in those early days. Hearst gave his friend Cissy Patterson one of these elegant horses. She kept it at her country home, the Dower House in Maryland near Washington, and she enjoyed riding, appearing for photographs, and visiting guests on her gleaming WAR CHIEF.

The Palomino registry requires a horse to be truly the color of a gold coin; only a scant shade darker or lighter is acceptable, and white markings are permitted on lower legs or face. The coat color of Palominos changes and darkens with age, but usually remains set by the age of six years. Their manes and tails must flash white, or nearly so. Sizes can vary from 14.2 hands to 16.3 but the color must be uniform. Breeding Palominos is an uncertain business, for crossing Palomino with other breeds or colors does not always produce Palomino. Palomino crossed with Palomino does produce a Palomino foal, but Palomino bred to chestnut could produce a chestnut or a Palomino. A Palomino bred to an Albino could produce either Palomino or Albino, but the color of that cross is often washed out and flat. All of which proves that genetics is a fascinating and complicated field.

While the Palomino registry attempts to set standards, it does admit that many different sizes and types can be true Palominos. The other club, the Palomino Horse Breeders of America, which began later, believes the golden horse not to be a breed or type but only a color.

After W. R. Hearst's death, the Palominos were sold, but today the Palomino has come back in glory to San Simeon. One of my husband's favorite mounts is a registered Palomino gelding, GALAGOLDEN GLOW, whom we call GLOW. He and my husband go together like peanut butter and jelly. GLOW is also in the Half-Arabian Registry. When my husband and I ride together and come to a dangerous or difficult stream or hill, GLOW always leads the other horses calmly and safely. He is wise and reliable yet dazzling in appearance.

As one visitor who saw him gasped, "Palominos are perfect!"

Chapter 11/The Arabians

My beautiful! my beautiful!
That standest meekly by
With thy proudly arch'd and glossy neck,
And dark and fiery eye;
The stranger hath thy bridle-rein—
Thy master hath his gold—
Fleet-limb'd and beautiful, farewell!
Thou'rt sold, my steed—thou'rt sold!

—Caroline Elizabeth Sarah Norton

*A*s early as 1919, William Randolph Hearst began to admire, ride, and breed Arabian horses. He plunged into breeding them on a larger scale in the 1930s when he purchased a number of horses from William Robinson Brown, president for many years of the Arabian Horse Club. Hearst said that he hoped "to improve Arabians in America, to supply other breeders with superior stock, and to perpetuate the pure Arabian blood."

Like all breeders, Hearst understood that the Arabian horse is unique and prepotent. Classified by some experts as a separate species—*Equus arabicus*—the Arabian is unique in many ways, His extra-large windpipe gives the Arabian great lung capacity, freedom from respiratory ailments, and stamina. Bred in the desert, he uses water efficiently and can go for long distances without stopping to drink. He has one less vertebra than other breeds, giving him a short, strong back. His wide-set eyes, narrow muzzle, compact barrel, high tail carriage, and especially his prepotency as a sire, all set him apart. Hearst also recognized that the Arabian is the fountainhead, the source of all light breeds of horses. The Quarter Horse, the Thoroughbred, the Standardbred, the Morgan, all owe their lineage to Arabians. Arabian blood was, as one horse historian, Herbert Reese, puts it, "the *quality* factor in the founding or improvement of existing breeds."

William Robinson Brown had obtained some of his Arabians from the North African desert and others from the Crabbet Park stud of Lord Wilfred S. and Lady Blunt in England. When Brown dispersed his celebrated Maynesboro Stud Farm in Berlin, New Hampshire, in 1936, W. R. Hearst and W. K. Kellogg bought most of his prize stock. GHAZI

ZAMAL OF PICO, one of Hearst's prize Arabian stallions

had been one of Brown's most important stallions. He was purchased by
Hearst for the San Simeon breeding program. GHAZI's sire *RODAN had
been imported from the Blunts' Crabbet stud; his granddam was one of
the horses bred by Ali Pasha Sherif of Egypt. GHAZI has had much influence on today's Arabians.

W. R. Hearst also purchased GULASTRA out of GULNARE.
GULASTRA's sire, *ASTRALED, was the horse that brought the MESASOUD
bloodline to America. MESASOUD, whose blood is known by Arabian
breeders throughout the world, had also been purchased from Ali Pasha
Sherif by the Blunts. And in the same dispersal sale, Hearst bought
GULASTRA's son, RAHAS, out of RAAD. Both GULASTRA's and RAHAS's
bloodlines consistently produced refined, well-built horses, larger than
average with exceptionally high action. RAHAS, in fact, is the ancestor of
more champions than any other horse in the GULASTRA line. RAHAS's
son RABIYAS sired ABU FARWA, a horse in the pedigrees of many outstanding champions. RAHAS's last son, born after the death of W. R. Hearst,
became our stallion RAHMOUN. A rich mahogany bay with well-placed
white markings, he carried eleven direct lines to MESASOUD and sired

a number of the Arabian horses of similar bloodlines, which we take pride in today.

Through additional purchases made with the advice of Albert Harris, another president of the Arabian Horse Club, Hearst continued to expand the San Simeon stables. Julia Morgan, the architect of the castle at San Simeon, designed new, enlarged buildings to house the horses. These stables after certain repairs and restorations are still in use today.

Perhaps it was super-salesman Preston Dyer (he had been General Patton's trainer) who persuaded Hearst in 1945, at the end of World War II, to consider organizing and funding an expedition to the Middle East to search for new Arabian horses to add to the American gene pool. After the war, the countries of the Middle East were in turmoil. Preston Dyer was to discover that buying good horses was like looking for needles in a sandpile. He had met Prince Fouaz of the Rualla Bedouin tribe at a United Nations conference in 1945. The prince said he would help and Mr. Hearst was willing to pay. The great adventure was planned.

Dyer knew horses from poll to pastern. Nevertheless, he asked that Mr. Hearst pay a veterinarian to accompany and advise him. Hearst suggested that his son George head the group, which also

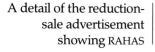
A detail of the reduction-sale advertisement showing RAHAS

included a photographer. When they reached Paris, son George wisely decided that he would rather look over the fillies on the Champs Elysées, so he stayed in France where he helped organize documents and shipping for the horses since the countries where they would purchase horses were under French rule.

Preston Dyer, in reminiscing, told me that he found no Arabian horses in Europe, even at the Blunts' Crabbet Park Stud in England, to equal those already in California. Once in the Middle East, he recalled, King Ibn Saud of Saudi Arabia, Prince Fouaz, and others were helpful. In Beirut, Henry Pharoun, the former French minister to Lebanon, assisted Dyer in looking for horses. They visited numerous Arab princes, sheiks, and tribes along the Euphrates River, and they sought out the celebrated Arabian horses of Sheik Ibn Muhayd and others.

By 1947, Dyer and Hearst had assembled fourteen Arabian horses, selected from more than three thousand. Six stallions and eight broodmares were to be shipped to California. Finding and buying the horses was difficult enough, but getting them to California proved nearly impossible.

Testimony to the power of money to smooth the way and to the stamina and endurance of the Arabian breed was the fact that while the world was still recovering from a devastating war, the horses made that hair-raising trip, which included twenty-eight days at sea in special stalls, a forty-eight-hour hurricane in which the boat almost sank, a cholera epidemic, a train trip by freight car across the United States, and lastly a fifty-mile journey by truck up the coast of California from San Luis Obispo to the Hearst ranch. The horses managed to survive that incredible voyage in fairly good condition.

The February–March 1948 issue of *The Horse Lover* magazine described the San Simeon stables importation as

> *one of the greatest shipments of Arabian horses ever to reach the United States; . . . climaxing a five and a half months search in the middle eastern countries of Arabia, Preston Dyer, Manager of San Simeon with John Williamson as photographer and Dr. Pulling as veterinarian arrived in California. The trip in search of the equine aristocracy took them approximately 25,000 miles to England, France, Italy, Tripoli, Egypt, Syria, Mesopotamia, Iraq, the northern Arabian desert and Lebanon. . . .*
>
> *Horsemen everywhere will rejoice to know that in America there reposes a goodly supply of that "eternal beast—the Arabian horse" not only a good horse in himself, but one whose blood has made other breeds great.*
>
> *America and the world owe a debt of gratitude to the owners and management of the San Simeon Stables for their most worthy contribution to this end.*

One of the young Arabians bred at San Simeon

The importations in 1947 were as follows:

Mares	Stallions
NAJWA #4206–gray	SNOUNOU #4205–gray
LAYYA #4208–gray	BOURHANE #4207–chestnut
KOUHAILANE #4209–gray	MOUNWER #4210–chestnut
LEBNANIAH #4211–gray	ARKANE #4212–brown
MANSOURAH #4213–gray	ZAMAL #4216–chestnut
RAJWA #4214–gray	GHAMIL #4217–chestnut
NOUWAYRA #4218–gray	
BINT RAJWA #4215–gray	

One stallion in the shipment, *ARKANE, was a gift from Henry Pharoun, and Hearst later sent the horse as a gift to the president of Mexico, Manuel Avila Camacho.

In 1948, as a bride, I first met Preston Dyer and visited the Arabian stables at San Simeon. For the first time in my life, I rode an Arabian horse. What an awakening! No, it was more like a dream. To ride such soft gaits, to know such a breathtakingly beautiful, responsive animal. From then on, I was hooked on Arabian horses.

Dyer's breeding plan involved using the desert-bred stallions on the American-bred mares that Hearst already owned, and crossing the desert-bred mares with his American stallions such as RAHAS.

A view of Pico Creek stable designed by Julia Morgan

No. 2357

The Arabian Horse Club of America
FOUNDED 1908
CERTIFICATE OF REGISTRATION.

Name ZIROAB *Color* Bay *Sex* Mare

Date Foaled April 17, 1942 *Markings* Irregular blaze; left front white to ankle on outside, and inside above ankle; right front fetlock and white nearly halfway to knee inside of leg; right hind halfway to hock; left hind heel to ankle and inside coronet.

Dam's Name Roaba *Reg. No.* 749 *Color* Bay
Sire's Name Ghazi *Reg. No.* 560 *Color* Grey

Bred By Hearst Sunical Land & Packing Corporation
San Simeon, California

In Witness Whereof, Attest:

_____ *President*
_____ *Secretary*

Issued To Hearst Sunical Land & Packing Corporation
San Simeon, California

January 5th, 1943

The Jockey Club
CERTIFICATE OF FOAL REGISTRATION.

(No. 42606)

ARAB

This is to certify that *the* Bay Filly *named* ZIROAB
by Ghazi (Arab) *out of* Roaba (Arab)
foaled April 17, 1942, *is duly registered by* **The Jockey Club.**
Marks: Star and broad connected stripe, touching both nostrils and extending down on upper lip; left fore pastern white, extending on ankle on inside; right fore ankle white, higher on inside in back; front, inside and back of left hind pastern white; right hind leg white halfway to hock, higher on inside in front.

Registrar *Secretary*

Issued to Hearst Sunical Land and Packing Corporation
New York, December 31, 1942

CERTIFICATE TO BE PRESERVED AND TRANSFERRED TO THE PURCHASER IF THIS HORSE IS SOLD.— RECORD TRANSFER ON REVERSE SIDE.

W. R. Hearst believed in the infusion of new blood, new genes to improve Arabians and other breeds in the United States, and no importation directly from the desert had taken place for many years. However, instead of sunrise, it was sunset for Hearst. At a time in life when most men would not have embarked on such an expensive wild-horse chase, he had spent a fortune and savored the experiment. He was eighty-two years old, but he always took a long-range view, scanning the far horizon where the sun was coming up.

When he died, the trustees and executors of his estate were confronted by obligations to the heirs to reduce expenses, for they were entrusted with preserving capital for his estate. In 1951, Mrs. Garvin "Bazy" Tankersley had not yet "invented" the dramatic Arabian horse auctions which are so successful these days. Therefore, the prices obtained for these valuable animals were incredibly low. Perhaps if the men who organized the Hearst dispersal sale had used the promotion and advertising channels available to them in the Hearst empire, the prices for the horses would have been higher.

The low prices realized at the sale in 1951 had a bright side, however. These excellent horses selling for low prices gave many small breeders an opportunity to start their own breeding programs. A wider circle of people would be able to know the Arabian horse. Horse people who already liked Thoroughbreds, Quarter Horses, or Morgans could learn about the adaptability of the Arabian and its ability to improve their favorite breeds.

Before the sale catalogue was prepared, the sons of W. R. Hearst chose the horses they wished to keep. Sons William and Randolph chose a select group on the advice of Richard Lynch, who had succeeded Preston Dyer as stud manager. I remember Lynch's words, "If you don't keep any other mare, keep MOUNIGHA. She's the best Arabian I've ever seen." Foaled in 1949, the same year our first son, William, was born, MOUNIGHA was another product of the desert-American cross. She had been sired by the imported desert stallion *MOUNWER; her dam was NIGHA; NIGHA was by ROABRA (a son of RAHAS out of GHANIGAT).

We also kept the gray mare *RAJWA, one of the desert horses, and Randolph kept a few of the desert mares. Bad luck plagued *RAJWA's offspring. Very difficult to settle in foal, she had only one surviving foal, NANNI, who inherited the same difficulty. However, my sons adored *RAJWA, who was their favorite, gentle, reliable riding horse. She taught them to love horses.

My husband and I persuaded a local horseman and rancher, Lloyd Junge, to look after our stable of Arabians. He stayed on for fifteen years, taught our sons, Willie and Austin, to ride, and trained the horses he had bred, foaled, and raised. ZAMIGHA, by *ZAMAL out of MOUNIGHA, he had made into a cow horse, our son Will's pet. MIDNIGHT (born at that hour, according to Junge), a granddaughter of RAHAS,

An impressive line-up of Arabian stallions at San Simeon: (left to right) JOON, RAHAS, SABAB, GULUSTRA, KASAR, and GHAZA

always gave us gorgeous foals, and her daughters are our prize mares today.

ZAMAL'S FRIENDLY *was* friendly, from the first moment she entered the world. She was still friendly at the age of twenty-five and once again in foal. She was another product of desert-bred *ZAMAL out of MOUNIGHA and spent her life beside Pico Creek, within earshot of the Pacific surf, in a pasture shadowed by rare Monterey pines (one of the last stands in the world) and California live oak. Her constant companion was her retired full sister, PICO LINA. Their daughters and granddaughters grazed in fields nearby. The story of FRIENDLY seems as good a tale for Disney as *The Black Stallion,* but perhaps I'm prejudiced. Because of FRIENDLY we made friends with Harry and Katie Harness, for twenty-four years our valued advisors.

That friendship happened because I was disheartened, as I often have been in the past thirty-five years, when I feel like getting out of our horse operation. In a conversation with Bazy Tankersley, another trusted friend of long standing, I asked her to recommend someone who would visit the San Simeon stables, survey our situation, make suggestions, and help us sell horses.

"Harry Harness would be my choice," she said without hesitation. "He's knowledgeable and totally honest."

Harry and Katie Harness, who had years before bought horses of Hearst breeding, thus came into our lives. They have helped so often over the years that memory fails to count the times.

We have always been amazed and pleased to find so many generous, happy people among other Arabian breeders. Instead of being close-mouthed and competitive, they are invariably eager to share

A chart showing the pedigree of the imported desert-bred stallion *MOUNWER

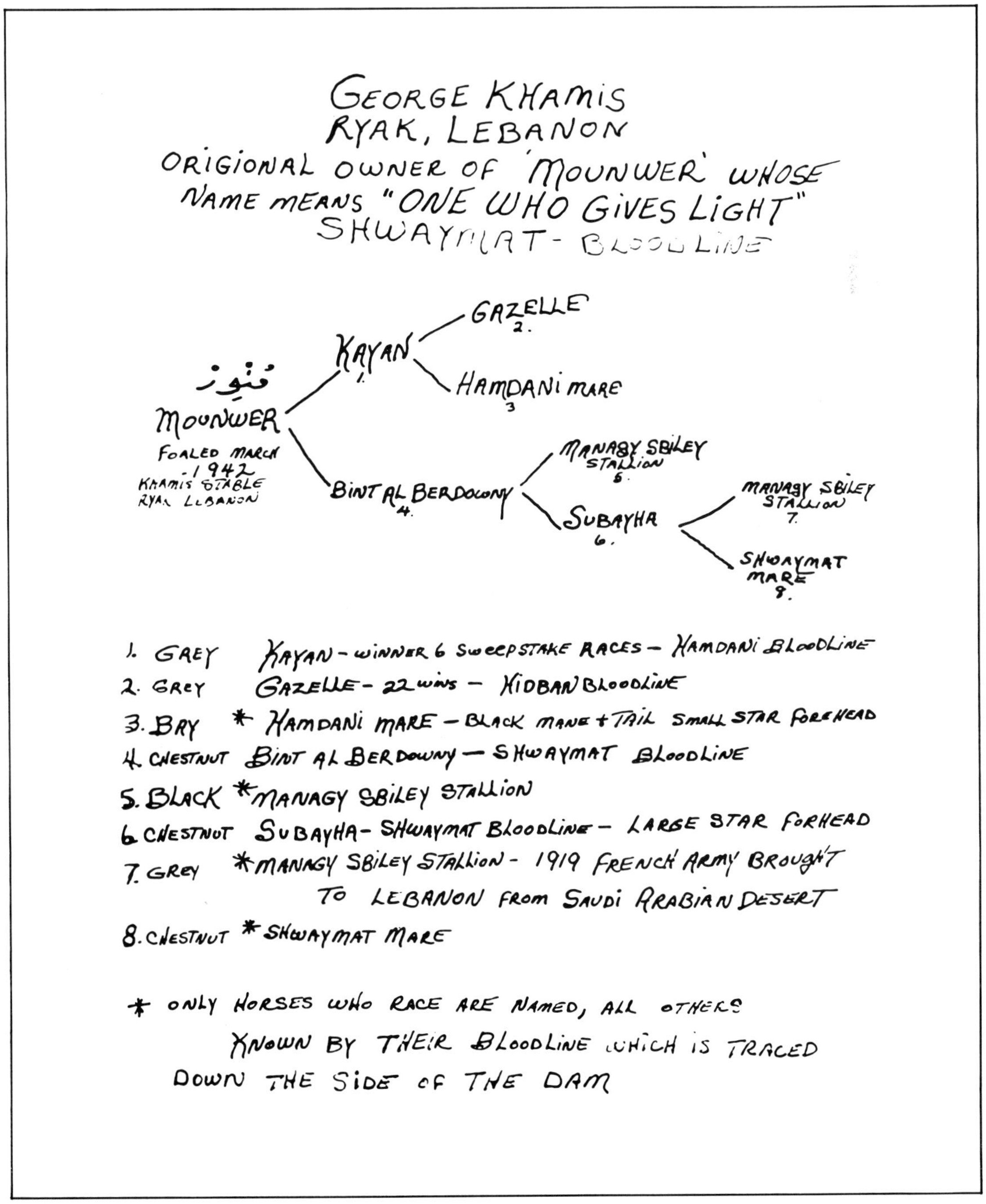

GEORGE KHAMIS
RYAK, LEBANON
ORIGIONAL OWNER OF 'MOUNWER' WHOSE NAME MEANS "ONE WHO GIVES LIGHT" SHWAYMAT - BLOODLINE

مُنوّر

MOUNWER
FOALED MARCH -1942
KHAMIS STABLE
RYAK LEBANON

KAYAN 1.
- GAZELLE 2.
- HAMDANI MARE 3.

BINT AL BERDOWNY 4.
- MANAGY SBILEY STALLION 5.
- SUBAYHA 6.
- MANAGY SBILEY STALLION 7.
- SHWAYMAT MARE 8.

1. GREY KAYAN - WINNER 6 SWEEPSTAKE RACES - HAMDANI BLOODLINE
2. GREY GAZELLE - 22 WINS - KIDBAN BLOODLINE
3. BAY * HAMDANI MARE - BLACK MANE + TAIL SMALL STAR FOREHEAD
4. CHESTNUT BINT AL BERDOWNY - SHWAYMAT BLOODLINE
5. BLACK *MANAGY SBILEY STALLION
6. CHESTNUT SUBAYHA - SHWAYMAT BLOODLINE - LARGE STAR FOREHEAD
7. GREY *MANAGY SBILEY STALLION - 1919 FRENCH ARMY BROUGHT
         TO LEBANON FROM SAUDI ARABIAN DESERT
8. CHESTNUT * SHWAYMAT MARE

* ONLY HORSES WHO RACE ARE NAMED, ALL OTHERS
     KNOWN BY THEIR BLOODLINE WHICH IS TRACED
  DOWN THE SIDE OF THE DAM

Mrs. Nicki McGinnis has been very successful in hunter classes with the Hearsts' mare HOSANNA PICO.

Mares and foals in front of San Simeon's Pico Creek

ideas, to give advice, and help. Of all the friends we have come to know through the horses, however, we cherish the Harnesses the most. They persuaded their friends Gene and Viola Whitten to buy FRIENDLY. They developed her into a champion many times over. The Harnesses and the Whittens had been breeding horses similar to ours, and we all decided to have a sale together in 1975. At San Simeon we arranged to build a show ring and put up a tent; we got the best auctioneer and offered thirty-one horses at public auction. We felt that the quality Arabians of similar breeding offered a rare chance for purchasers to obtain these bloodlines, backed by many generations of proven ancestors.

Prices at that sale can't be compared with the bonanzas brought in recent auctions, but we did meet and get to know many distinguished breeders. Among them we were particularly interested to meet Mr. and Mrs. George Khamis, who had moved to America from

Ryak, Lebanon. His family had been the breeders of *MOUNWER, whose name in Arabic means "one who gives light." Mr. Khamis gave us photographs and detailed desert pedigrees of the ancestry of *MOUNWER as well as other horses purchased from his family's stud during the Hearst 1947 expedition.

Gene Whitten felt that his own years were numbered after his wife, Viola, died and he knew he would have to part with every one of his horses. He was so heartbroken he could hardly talk when he telephoned to offer them to us. We bought his remaining horses, and thus dear old FRIENDLY returned once more to the fields of her birth at San Simeon.

RAHMOUN, the last son of RAHAS, was first broken, trained, and shown by Mr. and Mrs. Bob Smith, another fine horse family. The

MOUNIGHA and her colt, SEÑOR PICO, in the field at San Simeon

Saccoman

stallion became almost a house pet for the Harnesses who leased him from us, and when he died, a piece of Katie Harness' heart died with him. RAHMOUN's daughter POLAR gave us the gelding POLARIS, voted best Arabian Hunter of the Year by the American Horse Shows Association. A super "lepper" (as the Irish call a good, safe jumper), he makes a fine Master's mount when he carries me fox hunting as a Joint-Master of the Golden's Bridge Hounds. The only Arabian horse in our hunt, he has won the admiration of every member. Even the dedicated Thoroughbred owners have praised his steady, careful jumping and good manners. It gives me special pride to think that he is the fourth genera-

197

tion I have ridden. At San Simeon I first rode his great grandfather, RAHAS, then his grandfather, RAHMOUN, and his mother, POLAR. POLARIS continues a family tradition.

Horses are like types of liquor: all are good, but some are better than others. I believe one of the better Arabians is a mare, KISHTEE PRI MOUN, picked out for me by Harry Harness in order to buy back some of our old Hearst bloodlines. Her sire, MOUNRI, son of the desert-bred stallion *MOUNWER, was United States National Champion Top Ten Stallion. He had been sold at the San Simeon sale in 1951 and he certainly proved Dyer and Hearst were right in their breeding theory. My pet mare's dam, KISHTEE PRIZA, a granddaughter of *MOUNWER, was U. S. National Top Ten Park Horse.

At San Simeon stables we have not shown as extensively as we would have liked but we have bred, sold, and shown on a small scale and a careful budget. For the past ten years, under the knowledgeable management of Richard Skinner, we have produced a few foals to sell of similar historic bloodlines. We try to give first choice, not to the buyers with the most money, but to the ones we feel will add luster to the horses we have produced. Like Lady Anne and Wilfred Blunt at Crabbet Park, we have tried to breed a big, strong Arabian horse without losing type or refinement.

I like calm, kind, sensible horses, and, of course, I believe that conformation does mean good performance. A horse can move and do the job he is asked to do if he is built right. The standards established for Arabian horses perfectly describe a horse that will be useful for trail riding, showing, jumping, and traveling long distances, and yet will remain sound. I also feel that size matters. All things being equal, I have found for my purposes that a good, big Arabian is preferable to a good, small one. And so we will continue to breed for disposition, conformation, and size, in that order.

At San Simeon we will probably always breed Arabians, the oldest, purest-blooded, most beautiful breed in the world. For as the ancient Arab saying goes:

> *Allah created the horse out of the wind and he created Adam out of the mud.*

Part IV/ The Third and Fourth Generations

Chapter 12/Rides Out of the Past

If thou wouldst have me paint
The home to which, could love fulfill its prayers,
This hand would lead thee, listen...
A palace lifting to eternal summer
Its marble walls, from out a glossy bower
Of coolest foliage musical with birds...
And when night came... the perfumed light
Stole through the mists of alabaster lamps,
And every air was heavy with the sighs
Of orange-groves and music from sweet lutes,
And murmurs of low fountains that gush forth
In the midst of roses!—Dost thou like the picture?

—Sir Edward Bulwer Lytton

I first visited what was probably the most fabled private residence in America in the spring of 1945, after a newspaper assignment covering the formation of the United Nations in San Francisco. In those days I worked for a newspaper. My boss, the extraordinary Eleanor "Cissy" Medill Patterson, owner, publisher, and editor of *The Washington Times-Herald* and a longtime friend and onetime employee of William Randolph Hearst, had arranged an invitation for me to spend a few days at San Simeon after the San Francisco conference. Cissy told me there would never again be a place like San Simeon and that I should go to see it now. W. R. Hearst, the press lord who had alternately amazed and infuriated entire nations, was in his eighties. Some people thought he would be around forever. Cissy, who loved him, realized that he would not.

A car, sent by my host, met my train in San Luis Obispo, fifty miles from the Hearst property. For the last fifteen miles away we could see the castle on top of the mountain and for the last five miles we wound around the road up the mountain, passing exotic animals. We had to wait for the llamas and the kangaroos and the water buffalo to get off the road before we could continue. When the car finally drew up at the foot of a wide marble flight of stairs, the sun was sinking, a giant ruby set into the sea.

Everything I had heard about San Simeon turned out to

This picnic area on one of the hills was a favorite stopping place for Hearst and his riding guests.

be an understatement. Hearst's "Casa Grande" on top of a mountain at the end of five rather impressive twisting miles of manicured driveway was and still is an enchanted castle of immense size, in Spanish-Moorish style, garnished by towering palms, masses of flowers, and marble statues.

The vast terraces suggested nothing so much as Mount Olympus. Literally everything in sight with the exception of the Pacific Ocean belonged to Hearst. From almost any old carved balustrade you could gaze down on tens of thousands of acres of rolling pastures descending sensuously to the sea.

Nature had thoughtfully draped a shimmering mantle of brownish-gold grass over everything. Although this grassy gown was entirely natural, it looked glamorously contrived, like everything else. George Bernard Shaw once described Mr. Hearst's house as what God would have built "had he had the money."

An executive housekeeper, Ann Miller, met me and installed me in my quarters in Casa del Monte, one of the three guest houses that formed a half-moon in the gardens around the main castle. Had this guest palace stood by itself, say, in Beverly Hills, it would have been a local marvel. But up here on the Enchanted Hill one might almost have overlooked it.

There was, and still is, a famous room in Casa del Monte containing a bed reputed to have belonged to Cardinal Richelieu. Alas, they didn't put me there, but my own room did contain an antique four-

For the convenience of his friends, Mr. Hearst built a pergola large enough for three to ride abreast shaded from the hot California sun; the pergola extended for miles around the hills below the castle.

poster whose intricate carvings probably blinded an entire sixteenth-century Italian family. This bed sat on a very fine, very old Persian carpet, one of those with rich, aged reds and blues that almost glow in the dark. The complicated pattern of this rug looked simple in comparison to the carved, coffered, gilded, and painted ceiling above it. In fact, every surface in the Casa del Monte was thoroughly and exquisitely decorated.

The housekeeper tactfully outlined the host's wishes in a voice softer than the quail rustling in the gardens. Like most considerate hosts, Mr. Hearst left his guests alone. They could pass their time doing whatever pleased them, whenever it pleased them. Nothing whatsoever was expected of them except the obligation to assemble in the great hall before luncheon and dinner. Business associates and employees of the Hearst empire, however, were summoned to discussions between meals. Cocktails would be at eight-thirty, dinner at nine—an appropriate Spanish hour in a Spanish setting, I thought. Guests were expected to rise and appear fully dressed for breakfast, kept warm on a sideboard. Very English, I thought. Guests could drift in any time from eight until noon. Luncheon, also served buffet-style, was promptly at two.

In those days, no guides explained the collections of plants, animals, statuary, silver, paintings, Greek pottery, tapestries, rugs, furniture, medieval carved stone and wood doors, ceilings, choir stalls. I wandered around alone, half expecting to meet a ghost. Almost empty with only a dozen guests, the castle and gardens had a fairy-tale aura. It was both unreal and unbelievable.

At precisely 8:25 P.M., dressed now for dinner, I gave my makeup a final pat and set out for the Casa Grande. The vast terraces that separated my rooms from the main building of the castle complex were completely empty. I can still hear the click of my high-heeled sandals on the polished tiles. The only other sound was the soft sighing of the wind. After nightfall, the gardens were illuminated by electrified alabaster globes that cast a soft and mysterious light on the banks of flowers, clipped hedges, shadowy walls, and flights of shallow stairs. The marble gods and nymphs seemed to watch in silence from their dim bowers of palm and bougainvillea.

Suddenly I stopped in my tracks. Before me, soaring into the inky nighttime sky and bathed in vivid golden light, were the twin cathedral towers of the Casa Grande. It had a positively unearthly magnificence. Then, without warning, a cool fog rolled silently across the terrace. I was engulfed in a perfumed mist redolent of ocean spray and tropical blooms. In minutes the edges of the world became soft and indistinct. The alabaster lamps became fairy lights, bright dots in the centers of luminous golden halos. The silence was utter.

I was almost afraid to breathe. Then the low moan of a fog horn echoed up the hills from the shore below. That ghostly mist added to the enchantment. I literally had to tear myself away, prompted a bit, I'll admit, by the housekeeper's earlier warnings about Mr. Hearst's displeasure at tardiness. But at last I hurried from the mysterious foggy garden into the light and warmth of the great assembly hall for the ritual San Simeon pre-dinner drink. That first night in the assembly room, Mr. Hearst materialized from a concealed elevator door in the choir stalls. He did not have a cocktail, but he spoke to me for the first time since my arrival and dinner was announced in a few minutes.

When I met Marion Davies, I made a gaffe. "You were my mother's favorite actress!" I gushed, a remark that quite naturally was greeted with a rather cool look.

Marion Davies always sat opposite W. R. at the center of the long, antique refectory table, never decorated with flowers but with cat-

One of the guest houses at San Simeon

sup and condiment bottles. The host thoughtfully rotated the other guests in the seating each evening, so that each lady had a turn sitting as guest of honor on his right. Mr. Hearst had not accorded to Miss Davies the status of a hostess. She did not manage the household staff, order the food, plan the menus, or seat the table. He was the lord of the manor and she was like a guest of honor.

We were a jolly crew that night, small by Hearstian standards but talkative. There were just twelve of us, facing one another in the middle of the refectory table, which sat fifty-six. Hearst radiated satisfaction because he was back in his beloved San Simeon. He and his lady love, Marion Davies, had spent the war years hidden away at Wyntoon, a sort of Grimm's fairy-tale village in the dark mountains of northern California. (The government had convinced them that San Simeon was a sitting duck for prowling Japanese submarines, and its prominent situation above all that rolling real estate did lend credence to the idea. Fortunately nobody ever took a shot at it.) Foxy little Louella Parsons, the Hearst empire's irrepressible gossip columnist, and her husband, an M. D. and a two-fisted drinker, were also guests. The doctor, whose name was Martin, liked to close his evenings by announcing with a wink that he had to perform "brain surgery" in the morning. The group also included the Carringtons and the Coblentzes, couples whose respective husbands ran the *Los Angeles Herald* and the *San Francisco Examiner.* They were seated at one end of the table. Harry Crocker, a sleek and amusing bachelor of the sort who is always invited places, and W. R.'s twelve-year-old grandson, John Hearst, Jr. ("Bunky"), anchored the other end. Twenty feet of unused walnut tabletop extended away from us in either direction into the darkness like the wings of W. R.'s private DC-3.

This Gothic millefleur tapestry showing horses and hounds going out for the hunt decorates a wall of the billiard room at the Hearst castle at San Simeon.

Anyone who has seen the dining room—and about a million tourists go through it now each year—can just imagine how our little group was dwarfed by the immense height of the ceiling. How awesome it was to glance upward at ceremonial banners and the carved countenances of wooden saints staring back down at us. The complicated medieval event depicted on the tapestries that lined the walls were equally out of scale. Everything about San Simeon, as a matter of fact, was distinctly awe-inspiring. One felt transported to a long-ago time, to a place that had little to do with the real world, especially the disillusioned world of 1945.

Soon after dinner, Mr. Hearst and Miss Davies led the way into the private theater, trailed by their dachshunds and guests. I learned later that there had been a showing at six for the staff, which numbered about thirty. They had eaten their dinner at five. Now it was our turn to settle into the plush burgundy seats and enjoy the show. How can I convey the tingle of anticipation I felt going into that fantasy theater? Even the dimming of the house lights, bunches of tiny bulbs clasped by enormous gilded goddesses, was exciting!

213

Whether bored or called by nature, some guests stole quietly
out of the theater. Whether the movie was good or not the dogs stayed
faithfully on, piddling if need be on the carpet. After the movie, walking
back to my guest house, I noticed that the fog had become heavier than
ever. Again I couldn't help but pause on the perfumed path to marvel
at what lay around me. Could Los Angeles or New York or any place I
had been really exist on the same planet as this wondrous place? I slept
soundly that night and had exalted dreams.

The next morning I was to take a ride. My companion, and
indeed the one who had suggested the outing, was W. R.'s ebullient
grandson Bunky. Still a pudgy boy, he nonetheless showed ample
promise of becoming the amusing man he ultimately became. I was
sufficiently charmed to accept his invitation, and I was also curious to
have a closer look at the land.

This part of California looked utterly unlike the Virginia
piedmont where I had grown up, or the rocky eastern seaboard, or the
hard edges of the Midwest, or anything I had ever known. Behind the
distant hills rose craggy mountains wreathed with manzanita, live oaks,
and sweet-smelling bay trees. Maxfield Parrish himself couldn't have
painted the scenery any better.

In 1945, as now, I had a passion for horses and riding. I had not packed boots. No matter, W. R. kept a complete outfitting room. Little used at this date it still contained dozens of complete sets of everything from jodhpurs to boots to caps to hacking jackets to—you name it. There was probably no guest in the history of the place who had been too fat or too tall or too whatever to be outfitted here. All this riding gear was a souvenir of the twenties and thirties when W. R. and Marion invited the Hollywood film colony by the trainload for the weekend. I wondered which boots had been worn by Cary Grant and which were Gary Cooper's? Did Carole Lombard ride in a Western or an English saddle? I myself looked very fine indeed, I thought, emerging from Mr. Hearst's "horse closet." Feeling like a movie star, I strode to the edge of the terrace to meet Bunky.

The horseback picnics and campouts of earlier years were long past when I visited in 1945. Organized with particular care, those long rides had engendered wonderful stories about movie stars and V.I.P.'s suffering with blisters and aching muscles. Clark Gable, weary and sore but unwilling to admit he was not man enough to survive a particularly arduous day in the saddle, was said to have whimpered to Gary Cooper, "When we get to the brow of the next hill we'll see Los Angeles!"

David Niven quipped on one occasion that, "Trying to keep up with Mr. Hearst is harder that putting toothpaste back in the tube!"

Claire Windsor and Buddy Rogers, guests at the castle

When riders reached the picnic site, the less adventurous guests would be waiting, having been transported by trucks and cars with the butlers, maids, iced champagne, cold beer, and a sumptuous feast. Cowboys would attend to the horses. A portable kitchen would be set up by a large staff, who also set up the camp, chilled the wine, laid the silver and linen tablecloths, and put out the catsup and mustard bottles.

Someone asked Carole Lombard, noted for her earthy talk, what she had seen of interest on her ride. Mr. Hearst pretended not to hear when Carole, thinking she had cleaned up the word answered, "Well, I saw a couple of cows ... ferking!"

The riders would be led by Mr. Hearst and Don "Pancho" Estrada, one of the few who dared call William Randolph Hearst "Willie." Wearing a white linen coat, a stiff Castillian sombrero, English breeches, and hunt boots, Hearst often rode a Palomino horse in a Western saddle. In earlier times, his rides had sometimes lasted three or four days, but, of course, he never left his own land.

My mother-in-law, Millicent, W. R.'s long-suffering wife, told me that early in her marriage they had made a rugged ride from Monterey down to San Simeon, sleeping along the way wherever they could find shelter. Mexican guides led them on the mountain trails. One night

A star-studded group: Hedda Hopper, A. P. Gianini, Claire Windsor, Douglas Fairbanks, Sr., Mary Pickford, and others

she remembered sleeping in a cave. "It was full of bones and had a funny smell. An old codger we ran into later on the trail laughed at us. Told us that it was a well-known mountain lion den!

"The couple we started out with turned back after two days, but I stuck it out," she bragged. "That was not the *only* time W. R. ever lied to me," she winked. "He had told me it was a short ride!"

For a New York City girl, Millicent, who didn't know a crop from a croup, showed a stout heart and a tough seat. She always rode astride, in full-cut breeches and boots, since in the West sidesaddles were seldom seen. And she kept up with her vigorous husband on his Herculean rides and campouts. A letter Hearst wrote to his mother reveals his robust endurance as well as his wife's forebearance.

> *...up the coast for ten or twelve miles. We went last night up to Pat Garrity's [the name of a mountaintop] and camped. This morning the two youngest woke us up at half-past four.*
>
> *We had breakfast and then came down to the Arroyo de la Cruz and went in swimming in a big pool, first the children, then the girls, and finally the men.*
>
> *We are back at our regular camp at the top of the hill now [this is where the castle stands today] tired and sleepy on account of those kids. I love this ranch. It is wonderful. I love the sea and I love the mountains and the hollows in the hills, and the shady places in the creeks, and the fine old oaks, and even the hot brushy hillsides—full of quail, and the canyons full of deer. It's a wonderful place. I would rather spend a month here than any place in the world. And as a sanitarium! Mother, it has Nauheim, Carlsbad, Vichy, Wiesbaden, French Lick, Saratoga, and every other so-called health resort beaten a nautical mile.*

On that first visit of mine, of course, I didn't know anything about this family history of riding and camping. I felt exactly the way any tourist who visits the castle today feels—awed, wonderstruck, and curious. I knew, of course, that Mr. Hearst bred horses somewhere on the San Simeon property. After all, W. R. had once made Cissy the splendid gift of a prize Palomino at a time when they were true rarities. I had also seen Hearst cowboys galloping after cattle.

Typical of San Simeon there were three stables. The ranch hands kept their Quarter Horses down near the bottom of the long road in the vicinity of the hay barns and the private airstrip. But guests were given horses kept on the Enchanted Hill itself, in a forty-stall stable behind the Casa Grande.

The best horses—the champion Arabians and the golden Palominos—all grazed about ten miles away (still on the property, of course) at the area called Pico Creek. This latter stable still thrives in a hidden valley whose steep slopes are covered with ancient live oaks and rare Monterey pines.

Mr. Hearst and Don
Pancho at the castle

But on the morning in the spring of 1945 when I was a guest, the famous Appaloosas, Palominos, Morabs, and Arabians were not offered as mounts. What we got instead were, well … just horses. But one of them had a fine-looking English saddle, as I had requested. On my first ride at San Simeon, the horses were waiting for Bunky and me at the foot of the terraced garden steps. Bunky introduced me formally to "Baz" Villa, a wiry cowboy who bowed gravely, helped us mount, and accompanied us over the countryside.

Years later, I discovered that the erect, grizzled gentleman who sat his horse better than a grandee, who hopped down to open gates and sprang back into the saddle like a teenager, was then, in 1945 over eighty. At one time or another we've all met old people who are so energetic and alert, so physically fit, that their age seems an anomaly. So it was with our guide. His crinkled face, sun-baked to a leathery brown and wreathed with a polite smile, was decidedly the face of an old man. Yet his lithe body would have put most twenty-five-year-olds to shame.

For our ride that day with Baz Villa in the lead, we thundered across the hills, startling the occasional zebra and Asiatic mountain goat. W. R. Hearst had imported these and other exotics years earlier and allowed them to roam their own two-thousand-acre parcel at will.

Soon the castle had shrunk to a gleaming dot in the distance, crowning one of the hills. An hour later we were picking our way carefully along a narrow mountain trail. My heart pounded with exhilaration. Here I was in the secret part of a true private kingdom, led by a family retainer and trailed by a jovial young heir.

We threaded around massive tree trunks, our horses' hooves muffled by a centuries-old carpet of fallen oak leaves. Baz Villa evidently had a destination in mind. A saddlebag of sandwiches and cold drinks was to be our reward when we got there. But where was it, I wondered? What hideaway presided over by what magical woodland spirits would we finally find?

When I saw it at last, it was like everything else at San Simeon—grander and more enchanting than my wildest imaginings. A thin cascade of water plunged like a twisting rope of silver into a deep pool at the foot of a rocky cliff. Mossy boulders and the gnarled roots of ancient trees rimmed the pool. The air was filled with the smell of mountain ferns and pure water. If it had been open to the public, the place would have been a tourist attraction like Yosemite. Instead it was just another hidden wonder of the Hearst Ranch.

We savored our sandwiches like pilgrims in the presence of something holy. And in a way, we were. Being in that place at that moment was almost a religious experience. I could see why generations of Hearsts had so loved it. The land had a way of speaking directly to the heart. If ever there was something precious on the face of the earth, something whose preservation was worth fighting for, I realized then that it was this land, this incredible San Simeon.

This beautiful silver and gold parade saddle was made especially for W. R. Hearst by Edward H. Bohlin, who was the "Stradivarius" of saddle makers during the 1920s and 1930s, catering to Hollywood stars and potentates from all over the world. The saddle was stolen in recent years but is so unusual that it was actually recovered by local police.

Chapter 13/San Simeon Endurance Ride, 1976

> *... a dainty steed,*
> *Strong, black, and of a noble breed,*
> *Full of fire, and full of bone,*
> *With all his line of fathers known;*
> *Fine his nose, his nostrils thin,*
> *But blown abroad by the pride within;*
> *His mane is like a river flowing,*
> *And his eyes like embers glowing*
> *In the darkness of the night,*
> *And his pace as swift as light.*
>
> —Barry Cornwall

*O*nce only the idle rich could indulge in pleasure horses and participate in the sports of polo, horse shows, coaching, and fox hunting. Today in the United States, the largest club of any kind is the Pony Club. These clubs, along with 4-H Club training and suburban community stables, have attracted increasing numbers of children and adults of modest income levels to enjoy horse activities. Extra leisure time has been a factor, of course, but relaxation on horseback helps people survive the pressures of today's industrial urban life. Equestrian sports bring together large groups of riders to share the joy of natural surroundings, take pride in their horses, restore their health and peace of soul. In almost every part of our country, enthusiastic horse owners participate in the growing number of hunt clubs, horse shows, and competitive trail rides.

One of the most distinguished groups of trail riders takes its name from the early California custom of traveling from *rancho* to *rancho* on horseback. *The Rancheros Visidores*, with 800 members, including leaders in business, politics, and the professions, represents every state, every age, and every walk of life. A board of directors and the president, Mr. Trevor Povah, decide who gets elected to the much sought-after membership.

Trail-riding groups such as the Frontier Boys and the Sage Hens have regularly camped out and ridden at San Simeon Ranch. The Sage Hens include women of all ages, all sizes, and all professions. Each member may invite one guest to join in one of the rides and campouts, which take place in spring or fall and last at least six days.

On these annual rides, members care for their own horses, although a catering service provides luxurious dinners and breakfasts and packs a picnic lunch. When the Sage Hens last camped at Chileño (one of the areas on the Hearst ranch), the acting "Trail Boss," Mrs. Lou Dahlen, visited the proposed campsite and surveyed the riding route several days ahead to familiarize herself with the terrain, the distances, and the hazards. After each daily ride the women care for their horses, feed and groom them, and bed them down. Margi Rupp of Santa Barbara, in her eightieth year, rides all day with the robust rest of them and does her chores with teenage zest and vigor.

In addition to pleasure rides such as that one, endurance trail rides and competitive rides are held throughout the United States, and one of the most memorable of them took place at San Simeon in 1976. A competitive ride tests how well a horse and rider can negotiate various marked trails, while an endurance ride tests horses for time and condition over a trail for a long distance.

Phoebe Hearst Cooke and other riders of the Sage Hens club ready for a first day's ride.

The Vermont and Virginia 100-Mile Endurance Rides and the Wisconsin Kettle Moraine Colorama 100-Mile Rides do not compare with California's Tevis Cup. That ride, a hundred miles in one day, starts at a six-thousand-foot elevation in Tahoe City and ends in Auburn, California, after some of the most rugged stretches of terrain in the world. In memory of Lloyd Tevis, who took over and ran the Pony Express, his grandsons each summer award the Tevis Cup to the horse and rider who complete the hundred miles in the shortest time and in the best condition.

For the San Simeon Endurance Rides, one of fifty miles and a less demanding one of twenty-five miles, the routes to be ridden were laid out over a period of many days. The crew were helped and guided by Charlie Parlet, then the ranch manager. These grueling rides would wind from the shoreline up into the Santa Lucia Mountains, and down through the lush valleys.

Two days before the rides, however, there were record rain

PICO CREEK
endurance ride

Hearst Pico Creek Stables, San Simeon, California
Ride the beautiful Hearst Ranch—first time open to the public.

August 21, 1976

Travel through picturesque country with breathtaking views of the ocean and the beautiful Central Coast Mountains. You will pass through the Keystone Mine, Marmaleo Flats and Black Oak area, to name a few of the many historical sites.

All proceeds will be donated by the Hearst Corporation to and for the benefit of the Central Coast of California Arabian Horse Association, courtesy of Mr. and Mrs. William Randolph Hearst, Jr.

Awards Banquet Barbeque is included in the entry fee of $50.00, and there will be $1.00 drug fee.

Unique awards for Top Ten, Breed and Completion.

Excellent outdoor camping.

Entries close August 6, 1976
Check-in time is 12:00 noon, August 20, 1976
No Pre-Ride

Bring your horses . . . llamas and zebras!

CENTRAL COAST OF CALIFORNIA
ARABIAN HORSE ASSOCIATION

Sanctioned by the American Endurance Ride Conference and the International Arabian Horse Association.

Riders were invited to participate in the first endurance ride at San Simeon.

storms. Unheard of! It NEVER rains in California in August. Besides breaking records, the rain also broke the hearts of the hard-working men and women of the Central Coast of California Arabian Horse Association who had planned for months to stage this ride to benefit their organization. The rain washed out their careful markings of lime powder, which indicated the routes. Both trail rides had to be completely remarked. However, as horse show and trail ride managers know, if it has to be done, it gets done. One day before the event, over some of the roughest country in the West, working through the day and half the night, the new markings had been put in place. Riders and horse trailers from many states assembled the day before in the field near the Pico Creek stables. Each rider brought two or three helpers, advisers, and

224

kibitzers, who pitched their tents, sleeping bags, and trailers alongside the horses.

Before dawn's pink fingers stroked the brow of the hills, every person and every horse was stirring. The vultures, circling at sun-up watched the riders start north, just as Portola had done, up along the spectacular coast, toward the white rocks of Piedra Blanca.

Intent though they were on this torturous test of strength and stamina, the riders reported afterward their exhilaration at being the first to trailride on this land, never before opened to the public, viewing

Riders and helpers arrive at Pico Creek the night before the ride starts.

from horseback the castle set against the mountains and majesty of the mountains as the sun rose and gilded them.

At the first veterinarian's checkpoint, each horse was examined and its pulse, respiration, and general condition were cautiously evaluated. The riders got ready for a steep, rocky downward road to the valley of Burnett Creek, where the lunch stop would refresh them. The crews of helpers waited there anxiously for their riders to show up. The temperature had risen, as the riders descended into the streambed. Vets eliminated a few horses, realizing what a rugged ride lay ahead.

At the third veterinarian check, more horses were eliminated by the doctors. Those horses and their disappointed riders would have a long trailer ride down the mountain to the base camp at Pico Creek. But the riders who made it through that point headed jubilantly to the last leg of their race.

After seven hours, Bill Thornburgh, a rangy, stringy cowboy, and his rangy, stringy Arabian horse passed the finish line at a gallop. He shouted and waved his beat-up hat. Others followed, some at a walk, some at a trot, and some at a gallop over the finish line. The onlooking crowds yelled and cheered.

Weary horses were sponged and exhausted riders flopped down, groaned, smiled, and welcomed cool drinks and praise from their friends. Only after hours of cooling, rubbing, watering, feeding,

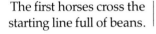
The first horses cross the starting line full of beans.

The first vet check was a welcome rest.

The fifty-mile mark

and bedding down the horses, did the riders and their helpers sit down to a steak dinner, served western barbecue-style by candlelight at tables on the lawn. A country band was the entertainment that night at Pico Creek. No food or drink ever tasted better, no music ever sounded merrier.

Bernice Kalland, 1975 Endurance Horsewoman of the Year, gives the camera a big smile atop COCHE, the 1975 Endurance Horse of the Year.

Kirk Levering, one of several Junior Riders, with his purebred Arabian Gelding GA-SOVEREIGN at Burnett Camp

◄ Mrs. Harlan Brown and Mrs. Lou Dahlen lead off the Sage Hens for a trail ride at San Simeon.

While riders, helpers, and spectators enjoyed their just rewards, poor Charlie Parlet, long after dark, with my two sons and other Good Samaritans, were back in the mountains in jeeps and trailers, struggling to pick up lost, exhausted, stranded riders and horses and haul them back to the starting point at Pico Creek. Luckily, when they all got back there was still enough steak left.

Horses climbing the hills with the Hearst Castle in the background

As Judy Selzer, reporting for *Saddle Action Magazine*, the trail-riders magazine, wrote in her article, "One of the most scenic endurance rides in the nation … added another dimension in the trail-riders' expanding horizon."

Voted "unique and unforgettable," the event, I understand, broke attendance records in the history of the sport for a first-time ride. It gave me a chance to see how much toughness, condition, and courage are required to compete in an endurance ride. But it also gave me a chance to share with those other enthusiastic riders the joy of riding over some of the most beautiful land in this country.

Chapter 14/Quarter Horses, Cowboys, and Cattle

Gonna saddle Old Paint
For the last time
And ride—
To the far away range of
The Boss in the sky
Where the strays are counted and branded
There goes I.
I'm headin' for the Last Roundup.

—Traditional Cowboy Song

*T*he castle may get written up and photographed and attract tourists, but the rest of San Simeon's land is still a working ranch. The cattle pay the taxes on the land, which stretches as far as you can see, in fact, farther than you can see. We must therefore understand and appreciate this cow business, the cowboys, their equipment, and their horses.

The Spanish method of cattle production changed very little after it was brought to the New World. In California, first under Spain and later Mexico, herds of cows, bulls, and calves ran wild as antelopes, free, unfenced, and managed by horsemen only occasionally. The Spanish breed of cattle were long of leg and drought-resistant, and had horns that measured anywhere from six to ten feet from tip to tip. The Spanish used only the cattle hides commercially for their famous leather, while the beef, milk, butter, and cheese were utilized for home consumption. When the hide and tallow (used for soap and other products) were taken from the skinned animal, the beef carcass often rotted where it lay.

Although those Spanish longhorns have been gone for years from California's hills, the Spanish terms have survived in the cattle-man's lingo: *lasso* for rope, *chaps* for leather pants, *corral* for pen. In Spanish cattle ranching, a gathering or *rodeo* of cattle took place once a year, in springtime, when the young were branded. At rodeo time the owners, their neighbors, and hired hands, or *vaqueros*, all camped out, and as they lassoed, branded, and castrated calves, they competed to see whose horses and lassoes were stronger and quicker, who could ride the craziest horse and throw the wildest calf. Thus were born the rodeo contests of today.

The Spanish rider seldom walked his horse. He trotted or galloped, whether going to work or riding for pleasure. In R. Guy McClellan's *Dictionary of the Golden State*, published in 1875, the author's accounts of Spanish horse breaking make it seem like a bone-breaking, hair-raising job. "The horses may be four or five years old," he writes, "having run loose, untamed and untouched."

After the horses were driven into a corral, one was selected, lassoed, tied up, and then blindfolded. A saddle was put on his back and he was then mounted by a *vaquero*. Terrified, he pitched, rolled, reared, and bucked until he was exhausted. This was the first lesson for a young horse. If he broke a leg or his neck, too bad; there were plenty more horses to choose from. In the next lesson, the horse was taught to help capture a cow. The cowhand threw one end of a rope over a cow's horns, and the other end was tied to the saddle. The horse was held firm while the cowhand dismounted and followed the rope to the cow. With his double-edged knife, he would cut the cow's tendons above the hooves of the hind legs to keep it still. Later, it was killed by plunging the knife between the horns to sever the spinal cord. Once the cow was skinned, the cowboy took the hide and the tallow for processing and perhaps some small part of the meat to eat for himself.

In 1855, a visiting Englishman named Frank Marryat returned

home to London and published his recollections of California's *ranchos*. He described a cowboy's dress as consisting of

> *a broad-brimmed hat, always secured under the chin, a loose shirt and jacket and buckskin breeches; round the leg is wound a square piece of leather, this is secured at the knee, and is a protection against falls or the attacks of cattle; in one of these leggings he carries his knife; his spurs, and lasso, complete his costume. The lasso is generally constructed of twisted hide, and is made with great care. In the hands of a good vaquero the noose is thrown carelessly, but with unerring precision; it is a formidable weapon of attack, and in the guerrilla warfare, which preceded the occupation of the country, it was not only used successfully, but horrible cruelties were practised by the Spaniards on those whom by chance they cut off in this manner.*

Marryat described the Californians as "perfect riders." Although their saddles were strange to him, he found them comfortable. At first he thought their crack riders would make a poor show on an English saddle over a steeplechase course, but he changed his mind. The Californians impressed him with their seats and the beautiful way they handled their horses' mouths.

Marryat wrote how the proprietor of the ranch kept open house for the roundups, and how the cowboys adorned themselves "in all their finery." At dusk the men, who had been drinking brandy all day as they managed the cattle, celebrated with a *fandango*, which usually ended with "knives being drawn and a letting of a little blood."

Marryat commented that it was "the nature of man to boast of his horse in all countries, and how unfortunate it is that these Spaniards are not sufficiently civilized to settle their disputes with a bet … and the whole would be decided in a gentlemanly manner."

After gaining independence from Spain and Mexico, the ranches under the American flag began selling their cattle for beef instead of their hides. By the time of the Gold Rush, the miners and settlers wanted fresh meat, so cattle were herded miles and miles to be butchered. Although both California and Texas had become American by 1850, cattle ranching still involved grazing the animals on vast, open, unfenced ranges, watered with streams and natural springs, and long drives over mountains, prairies, and rivers to market. Even though refrigerator ships and the canning process existed by 1879, beef cattle from the Hearst ranch were still rounded up and carefully driven fifty miles to San Luis Obispo to provide fresh beef on the hoof, a practice that continued until the twentieth century.

Whether they were Spanish, Mexican, or American, the early cowboys were real nomads and they were usually dirty, exhausted, financially impoverished, and lonely as they drifted from job to job and

The bunkhouse | ranch to ranch. Yet they became romantic heroes of fiction, movies, and the imagination. They are still popular ideals, representing all that is masculine, self-reliant, honest, and good. A cowboy could rarely hope to become an owner of land and cattle, for only rarely did he make good. But he had a sense of independence and self-importance, and he felt a camaraderie with the other ranch hands. In a sense, the bunkhouse resembled a man's club. The cowboy also felt himself to be an equal with the owner, an attitude that may account for his always walking tall.

Even after the introduction of barbed-wire fencing, around 1874, branding and roundups continued. In the past, many owners had shared the same unfenced grazing lands, and at roundup time, branding established ownership of the cattle. Fencing meant that brands were not as important; as the holdings of land became smaller, breeding could be controlled since the cows and bulls could be separated. At about the same time, windmills were also invented, and water supplies could also be improved. Now the cowboy spent much of his time with wire, fence posts, pliers, and pitchforks instead of reins and lasso ropes.

Changes in the cattle business continued to be made slowly from 1880 to 1900. When the railroads reached California, the long cattle drives got shorter and shorter. Today, cattle are simply sold to feed-lot operators, who send trucks to pick them up in San Simeon as yearling animals. Cattle are bred to mature at an early age, and the stockman tries to keep his cattle from losing valuable weight.

Although cattle trailers, tractors, trucks, and jeeps have largely replaced horses on most cattle ranches, at San Simeon, a last stand of the true cowboy, the stock horse is still indispensable. A cowboy simply has to be on a horse to lead and guide steers, bulls, cows, and calves down from rocky, roadless, brushy back country to a corral. And in working among animals, namely cattle, the cowboy is best on top of another animal, the horse. Cattlemen insist that the Quarter Horse has more ability to work cattle than any other breed. As Robert Kleberg of the King Ranch wrote about the Quarter Horse, "He stops and turns easily and does not become leg-weary or lazy even when asked to stop and start quickly many times in the course of the day's roping, cutting or other work." To turn or catch a calf, this breed has a jet of speed. He can

Out to work the cattle

run with three hundred pounds of saddle and man on his back. He can turn, dodge, and duck at full speed and has the temperament to stand quietly even after fast action under stress.

The quality of the horses at the Hearst ranch has improved under the management of Jack Cooke, who is in charge with George Hearst, Jr., of the Hearsts' California property. Both Cooke and Harlan Brown, who looks after the cattle operation at San Simeon, are Quarter Horse admirers and have used the blood of such well-known sires as DOC BAR and POCO TIVIO. Both Cooke and Brown know that first-class horses enable fewer men to work faster. The modern ranch, a so-called "cow-and-calf" operation, always has too few men and too much work.

Exactly what is a Quarter Horse? Any animal having consistent and recognizable inherited characteristics can be called a "breed." Strictly speaking, the word "breed" can also mean a domestic animal registered in a pedigree book. There was no pedigree or stud book of the American Quarter Horse until 1940, although, of course, private owners faithfully kept their records. In the eighteenth century, the unique characteristics and conformation of the American Quarter Horse, which make him a *sprinter* rather than a *stayer*, were observed and written about. The racehorses at colonial America's smaller tracks, in fact, were more like Quarter Horses than Thoroughbreds. The Quarter Horse has thick muscles up front and thick, developed hindquarters. His tail is lower than the point of his hips. Heavyset, 14 to 15 hands high, the racing Quarter Horse and the longer-distance Thoroughbred share closely related ancestors. In fact, the Thoroughbred and the Quarter Horse breeds are closely intertwined throughout their history, and both owe much to the blood of the Arab and the Barb or Spanish horse.

No description of the Quarter Horse, the most popular American horse with more registered horses than all other breeds combined, could be written without consulting the foremost authority, a founder of the American Quarter Horse Association. I mean, of course, California-born Robert Moorman Denhardt, for years the editor of *The Western Horseman Magazine.* His carefully researched books are the bibles of believers in the Quarter Horse's past history and future potential. The following is a paraphrase of Robert Denhardt.

When ridden freely on a loose rein, a Quarter Horse can gallop in a tight circle, leaning over at an angle, almost touching the ground without losing balance. He can do figure-eights at a gallop, stop on a dime, pirouette on his hind legs, and do a complete right about.

A Quarter Horse can cut a steer out of a herd of cattle, and he seems to know what the steer will do next. He will keep nose to nose, twisting and turning to prevent the steer from rejoining the other cattle. That is the cowboys' ideal horse.

Next, take the evolution of the cowboy's saddle. It started in Spain and arrived in the New World with the Conquistadors. The Spanish saddle in turn can be traced back to the Moors who conquered Spain. And the Spanish saddle took something from the knights who had to sit in armor on horseback, legs down straight.

William the Conqueror in the Bayeux tapestry rides straight-legged, a long stirrup, a high cantle in back and a high pommel in front, which gave soldiers on horseback both protection and security. Of course, if you want to go back even further, Roman warriors are depicted on horseback, sitting astride, without saddles. Only *ladies* used saddles; in fact the word "saddle" derives from the Latin word *sella*, meaning chair.

Well into the 1960s cowboys still rode a basically Spanish or Mexican saddle. Pony Express riders used an invention called a *man-chilla*, a fitted leather cover large enough to cover the saddle frame, pommel, and cantle. This leather cover with its attached saddlebags could be quickly and easily lifted off and thrown over a fresh horse. Until the twentieth century, riders sat straight up in the saddle, their legs down straight for security and comfort. Riders raced and jumped like that, pushing feet forward, until Ted Sloan, an American jockey, found that if he made his stirrups shorter, lifted his weight from his buttocks to his knees and feet, his horse could gallop faster. Later, the Italian riders

invented the so-called "forward seat," with stirrups not so short but still putting the rider in balance *over* the saddle, not down on it. Most Olympic riders today use a modified version of the Italian seat, sometimes deep in the saddle, sometimes forward, taking their weight off the horse's back. The cowboy saddle, however, has not changed too much in the twentieth century. The pommel, or horn, and cantle are lower and stirrups adjust with buckles instead of leather laces, but these are only minor improvements. The cowboy still sits down in the saddle, his knee-caps over the stirrups. Stirrups are long and he sits to the trot, rather than posting. The reins are held slack; the slightest pressure on the reins directs the well-trained cowhorse.

The management of cattle, in other words breeding, raising, feeding, doctoring, selling, and shipping, has also changed somewhat at San Simeon over the years. Horses are now trailered to various locations. Cowboys still ride from dawn to dusk, but now they often return by pickup truck and horse trailer to sleep at houses provided by the management, where their wives and children can greet them. In the past, cowboys were usually young single men, willing to sleep out on the range; they lived, when not camping out, in a common dormitory, or bunkhouse, with meals provided by their employers. Today, however, most cowboys are married and the bunkhouse has been closed down.

There have been two bunkhouses at San Simeon. The first one, I remember, was a wooden out building near the old ranch house complex built by George Hearst around 1878. The first bunkhouse, designed in the same Victorian style as the main house, was two stories high and had many small bedrooms. Meals were served at a community table in a large room at the back of the main house. It was nothing luxurious but more comfortable than camping out on the range with bedrolls and chuckwagons.

After 1920, when W. R. Hearst inherited San Simeon from his mother and started building his castle, he commissioned the architect Julia Morgan to build a large Spanish-style bunkhouse which has now been remodeled into a guest house. It can accommodate visiting cattle buyers, ranch guests, grandchildren, or Hearst editors. The faraway parts of the ranch are visited often, of course, in jeeps and pickup trucks, so the cowboys need not live far from roads, schools, and stores as they once did.

Since I first visited the ranch, more than forty years ago, I have been learning the locations of the branding corrals and camps, their histories and origins of the names.

• Burnett Camp, nestled back in the hills behind the castle, bears the name of a family that leased the area in 1864 from Juan Castro, who was married to a widow inheritor of the grant of Piedra Blanca ranch.

• San Carpojo, sometimes spelled San Carpoforo, derives

Charlie Parlet, a cowboy
for sixty years

from El Karpophorus, a Greek word for "fruit-bearer," probably named by some learned early traveler because of the fruit orchards located there.

    • Chileño Camp was the property of Juan Chileño, a homesteader whose holdings were bought by George Hearst.

    • Marmalejo Camp recalls Frederico Marmalejo, who lived there. The same is true for Gomez Spring, named for Frank Gomez.

    • The Black Oak area designates a creek by the same name.

    • Middle Ridge, now at the southern end of the Hearst boundary, was formerly in the "middle," when the southern Santa Rosa Ranch was owned by George Hearst.

    To these widely scattered areas, miles apart, crews of cowboys would be sent in the old days to eat and sleep out with their horses and chuckwagon, to brand, doctor, and gather cattle. With exactly the same anticipation farmers show at the time of the harvest of their produce, ranchers and cowboys harvest their calves in the last roundup before sales. Some aspects of that roundup have changed over the past fifty years. The hard riding is the same, and the cattle must still be found and guided gingerly to holding pens. In the past, however, the ranch horse was less gentle than he is today. To catch him, the cowboy usually had to rope him. Today, however, the cowboy walks to the corral, picks out his horse, bridles him, and quietly leads him back to heave his stock saddle on him.

In the past, the cattle had to be driven many days to the markets or to train stops. Today, giant trucks and trailers drive to the ranch. The cattle are weighed, loaded, and shipped without having lost excessive weight. They are sent to feedlots to be fattened to become tasty hamburgers and steaks.

Branding every animal was essential in the old days when fences were few and rustlers were plentiful. Ranchers today still brand livestock. Thousands, in fact, pay an annual fee to retain their registered brands, which constitute the heraldry of the Old West. Even now California ranches must by law employ a means of identification for their cattle. In addition to their brands, some ranches use an ear mark or a tag of some kind, for cattle thieves still do operate and cause losses in the cattle industry.

In San Luis Obispo until 1917, the brands were registered on pieces of leather filed in the county seat. As I mentioned earlier, the missions introduced branding from Spain. The long _3 of Mission San Miguel represents the Trinity. The Hearst ranch has several registered brands: ℬ for Piedras Blancas. H and ₲H for Hearst ranch. The © belongs to another property in San Luis Obispo County purchased by the Hearsts some years ago, the Jack ranch.

The old brands and old ways, however, were not forgotten by old-timers such as the late Charlie Parlet, who came to the San Simeon ranch early in this century. His friend Emmet Reilly, who started to work about the same time, became in turn, cowhand, chuckwagon cook, and later chef at the castle. To have known these two men is to have experienced history on a great ranch of the Old West.

For example, the old-time chuckwagon was like home to a saddle-weary cowhand in bygone days. The chuckwagon cook was a combination doctor, mother, wife, and preacher. It was easy to pick up a bunch of working cowhands but a good cook was a treasure, rare to find. Like as not, he had been a cowboy himself so he knew the appetites of the men.

"The cowboys often graded a ranch," Charlie Parlet explained to me, "on the kind of meals the management provided. Rotten food, it was a rotten outfit to work for."

Only a greenhorn kid would disagree with the cook. The cook was the despot of the pots and pans. Absolute ruler of his wagon, he was responsible for cooking and serving three meals a day to a ravenous crew of buckaroos. Quite a feat it was, too, without an icebox or kitchen stove or any modern appliances. Besides chopping wood to build fires, he created meals from dried or canned provisions and root vegetables. His drinks and butter were kept in a stream. The food box of the chuckwagon was constructed at the rear end of a spring wagon. Essentially a large wooden crate, it had compartments for cooking pans, another for cups, plates, and cutlery. The back folded down to form a work table. Thus was the whole kitchen loaded onto wagon wheels.

At some of the camps on the ranch, a barbecue grill, a stone chimney, and wooden tables were built, but at other spots the cook had to assemble rocks as a base for starting a big fire. He would carry two iron bars to stick in the ground beside the fire with a crossbar on top to form a rack from which to hang his pots and Dutch ovens.

One of the chuckwagon cooks, Emmet Reilly, has recounted some of his memories for me. He came to San Simeon as a young buck and worked as a cook for the cowboys. An inventory of some of the supplies stowed away in his horse-drawn chuckwagon (later a truck) included butcher knives and saws, dishpans, soap, towels, an alarm clock, sugar, syrup, spices, catsup, mustard, pickles, chili powder, rice, noodles, potatoes, onions, dried and canned fruit, and vegetables by the case. There were also cases of coffee and canned milk, sacks of flour, sides of bacon, nails, horseshoes, hammers, bits of leather for harness repair, bandages, medicine, and Lord knows what else. Of course, beef in every form was butchered, cut, served, stewed, fried, and roasted by him. When calves were castrated, their testicles became a favorite dish called "Mountain Oysters."

As Dan Moore, author of many books on the American cowboy, writes about chuckwagon cooks, "…long since faded into the smoke of his cooking fires…he will never fade from the memories of the cowboys he fed and took care of…his boys." Emmet Reilly fitted this description like an old boot. After cooking outdoors in all weather and all conditions for all sorts of men, he finally became cook in the castle kitchen for W. R. Hearst, and later still for Will and me, and our two sons and assorted guests and dogs. He fed us all. He even saved flies to feed to our son Austin's pet turtles. Assisted by the housekeeper, Bertha Hawley, he pretended to enjoy packing up for our many campouts and picnics over the ranch. He and Bertha worked as a happy team for many years. With his pink cheeks, twinkling smile, and thick white hair, Emmet resembled a thin, jolly Santa Claus, giving out good food and Irish wit to all. He bubbled with dry humor and nostalgic stories, was endlessly resourceful, unflappable, unforgetable.

His friend Charlie Parlet, who also started to work for the Hearst ranch as a boy, stayed for sixty years, finally becoming the manager. Low-voiced and weather-beaten, Parlet looked more like a cowboy than Clint Eastwood or any of the men in cigarette ads. The sight of Charlie Parlet at the age of sixty-eight in a steer-roping contest, sitting his saddle straight as an Indian, was something I will never forget.

In the nineteenth century the branding chute came into use, so that roping and tying calves are now performed at rodeos more than on the ranches. Although some ranches still brand in the old way, most use of the calf chute, which can be run with fewer men. Charlie, however, kept up his roping ability and turned his talent into a hobby. He and Jack Cooke, who is married to George Hearst's great-granddaughter and who manages all the Hearst ranch property, used to travel together to various roping contests, which they won with ease.

Charlie would hold the coils of his lasso in his left hand with the reins, and the loop would be held, correctly, with the right hand. When he nodded to the judge that he was ready, the cattle chute on his right hand opened and out would charge a big steer. Charlie and his horse had to wait until the steer was twenty-feet across the arena before they leapt forward and caught up to the steer. Parlet's right hand would circle up, whirl out, and drop precisely over the horns of the steer. He did it quicker and more accurately than any of the younger contestants. They were young athletic fellows, but Charlie had been roping cattle on the range for fifty years.

A cavalcade of horses
and carriages trans-
ported the Hearst family
and government VIPs to
entertain the President of
Austria at San Simeon.

"Roping was part of the job and I had to teach it to the younger men," Charlie remembered.

"How did you first start working on a ranch? I asked one evening as we sat around the fire at our Pico Creek cottage.

"Learned to ride when I was six. Learned to rope by watching others, helping neighbors, near where I was born. I was born at an old stagecoach stop in the town of Pleyto in Monterey County. My father was William Parlet and he was a grain farmer. The stage horses need lots of grain. The town of Pleyto was about eighteen miles from Bradley. But it's gone now. Covered by Lake San Antonio." Charlie lit a cigarette. He had filled a paper with tobacco, rolled it, and closed it with a lick while he was talking.

"I was raised near the Hearst ranch," he went on. "I just came over the hill and asked for a job. I knew what to do because I was raised in it. What keeps a cowhand on is being willing to do anything. I've had a good life, outdoors with horses and cattle. Never owned a pair of shoes. Spurs, boots, broad-brimmed hats and blue jeans, they're my work uniform. Been riding for seventy years. Ridden more miles on horseback than in a car. Four-wheel drive can't replace the horse in our country. Too rough. Too brushy. We must have horses to find, gather, and pen our cattle."

"What's the difference between a film cowboy and a real cowboy?" I asked him.

He chuckled and leaned back. "Cowboys don't carry handguns for one thing. When I started, a rawhide lariat and grass hemp rope were standard. Today, nylon is used. It's stronger and coils better. There's a new breed. Cattlemen today are better educated. Production methods have changed. For instance, we use electric branding irons.

"But cowboys never carry handguns like you see in the movies or on TV. We may shoot a rifle during deer-hunting season, but very seldom does anyone shoot from a horse. I never carried a sidearm and I am an awful poor shot with a handgun. Another thing, we get home early. We run over five-thousand head of cattle. We brand a couple thousand calves a year. When you're in the saddle, outdoors ten hours, you're ready and glad to sit down and watch a western film on TV."

Charlie deserves a book devoted to him.

When he died, a chapter of the old storybook West closed forever. No one will ever know the ranch better than he did. He remembered every foot of ground, every tree, every spring, every gully, every fence line on a 100,000-acre spread. He had a lust for good food, good drink, good horses, good cattle, good friends, good family ties, all priceless attributes in a leader. Leadership counts as much as experience, knowledge, and courage to run a ranch as immense as San Simeon. Charlie's men and his horses always cooperated with him perfectly. They loved him and he loved them. But of all his deep loves, he loved most the ranch where he spent sixty years working, teaching cow lore to green young men, and teaching green, young horses to stop when the loop is thrown, to face the steer or calf, to keep a tight rope. Charlie understood cows and horses as well as he understood men. He had character, proving true what that other great roper, Will Rogers, said, "The outside of a horse is good for the inside of a man."

Since my husband brought me as a bride to San Simeon thirty-six years ago, I've known each of the managers of the ranch. Will's cousin, Randolph Apperson, was the manager for many years, during Will's father's time and ours. He was the son of Phoebe Apperson's

Native Californians Lassoing a Steer by Augusta Ferran

brother, Elbert, and therefore, the nephew of Phoebe and George Hearst and a first cousin to their son, William Randolph Hearst.

I became a fast friend of Randy's and of his wife, Frances. He used to chuckle with us over the many rides and horseback camping trips he had organized and supervised for cousin Will and his celebrated

Harlan Brown and friend

guests. The editors, the politicians, the heads of state, and the movie stars were often rotten riders who had to be nursed, coddled, and above all mounted on dependable, quiet horses.

"I often had to send out a crew to take rocks out of the trails and cut down limbs so they wouldn't bump their famous domes. Difficult bulls had to be removed too. But in all those years we had no casualties," Randy once boasted. He lived in the old ranch built by his Aunt Phoebe and Uncle George. Although he often spent weekends at his own ranch in Pleasanton, California, he too, genuinely gave his heart and work to the San Simeon property.

The present manager, California ranch-bred Harlan Brown, typifies the modern, sophisticated, professional cattleman. Although the brawny, sun-baked Brown can ride and doctor a horse or a cow with the best of them, he spends most of his long days—from sun-up to sunset—in his four-wheel-drive truck, inspecting fences, or feeding and watering cattle. He must also handle big tractors to clear the roads so that cattle can be driven to pens for culling, veterinary treatment, and inspection.

One afternoon with me, Harlan eased his large frame down into a Victorian chair in the parlor of the ranch house built by George Hearst. In a characteristic cowboy gesture, he neatly placed his wide-brimmed hat under the chair between his boots. We were going to talk about the cattle operation. As I questioned him, our conversation wandered over many phases of bovine life. He spoke of his cows fondly, almost as if they were lovely ladies.

"We've done some crossbreeding of our White-Faced Hereford cows with Angus and Brahman bulls. The crossbreds have fewer eye problems. Black cows don't have light-pink eyes. The crossbreds seem to gain faster. We buy our bulls from ranchers who specialize in breeding bulls. We try to breed to the best. While weight gain is important, ease of calving and disposition count, too. We always handle them easy.... We feed protein blocks and extra hay if it's a bad feed year. We must truck calves from San Simeon to our Jack ranch after we wean them. They run there until sold as yearlings."

The Jack ranch, more than seventy-three thousand rolling acres, lies over the hills, inland, east of Paso Robles, California. It was acquired by the Hearst Corporation some years ago from the Jack family who had in turn owned it for generations. Some fifty miles from San Simeon, it, like San Simeon, was once part of mission lands.

"We use dogs to help us gather the cattle," Harlan continued. The dogs move the cows to men on horseback. But they move them slowly. Herding cows requires a rider to be alert. Anything can spook the bunch and off they go. If *your* attention wanders, they'll wander."

The Hearst ranch uses dogs of medium size, generally black with some white markings. They have short hair, better for going through brush because they don't pick up burrs and stickers. Harlan told me the breed originated in Australia and carries a good deal of Border Collie blood.

I realized that it was hard for Harlan to explain the cattle operation to me. I knew so little that he had to start from scratch. I suggested that he outline the important points in the form of a calendar year, a Cow Calendar, and here is how he did it:

January, February, March

California cattlemen hope for good rains to make green feed. Everything depends on the weather. During these months, most of the cows will have their calves on the ground, though a few might be late. Bulls will have been put out with the cows in late December.

In March, weather permitting, cows and calves are brought in from the different ranges. The young bulls will be castrated, de-horned, and vaccinated. There are new vaccinations to protect calves against many diseases. A cow who has no calf is held apart; she is called a "dry cow." After a pregnancy check indicates that she is carrying a calf, she will be put in a field near the ranch headquarters to calve. After this late group has calved, they will probably not be re-bred until next season. A cattleman's goal is to have most of his cows "drop" their calves in a short period of time. If a cow is *not* with calf, she will be sold. The other cows and calves are put back on the ranges they came from.

April, May, June

These months are devoted to the same work as the months before. Because of the size of the ranch and the many areas that are steep, rough, and brushy, it takes a long time to get some animals in. And if weather has been severe, some of the roads are too torn-up to travel. By June, the grass begins to dry. We continually check on the feed.

Our cows are sold to buyers as slaughter cows, a uniform bunch of good, fat cows ready to go to a processor. Trucks come to San Simeon to pick them up. Feed-lot cattle buyers come to the ranch to pick up heifers and steers and truck them to their feed-lots to be fattened. The best heifers are kept as replacements for culled cows. These replacements will be bred in their second year of age. Angus bulls are used for this first breeding since the Angus bull generally produces a smaller calf at birth. After a gestation period of about nine months, these heifers as three-year-olds will have their first calves.

Harlan Brown with some of the cowhands and cattle

July, August, September

Cows and calves again are gathered, and weaning starts. Old or unsound cows are sorted out to sell. For ten days or two weeks, calves will be fed a good alfalfa hay. After they are weaned and quiet, they are moved to the Jack ranch to grow and fatten before being sold.

The remaining cows, young and old, after being checked out for veterinary problems, are returned to their San Simeon pastures.

October, November, December

Rains begin again. Grass gets green again. Cows get fat again and prepare to give birth again. And the whole miraculous cycle begins again.

Harlan Brown, a first-class contemporary ranch manager, is direct and hard working. He does not ask his men to work harder or longer than he works himself, and he meets his many difficult challenges head-on. He must get cooperation from a staff of good ranch hands. His employees, permanent and part-time, come in various ages, sizes, sexes, weights, and colors, ranging from welders, gardeners, auto mechanics, painters, housekeepers, horse breakers, carpenters, cowboys, to blacksmiths and security guards. He must also get along with neighbors, with tourists, trespassers, officials of the state, the federal government, and his Hearst Corporation superiors, as well as members of the Hearst family. Whether he is welcoming visiting V.I.P. guests, such as the president of Austria, or explaining a cow's udder to a five-year-old Hearst grandson, Harlan is the soul of diplomacy and discretion.

Nevertheless, Harlan loves his work and he is backed up by his equally dedicated wife, Missie, who shares his problems and feels exactly the way he does. Harlan Brown respects the land and the role of animals who must produce so the land can be conserved. He has a grand tradition of more than a century to carry on and live up to. He wears the crown of this kingdom of San Simeon ranch with real pride and a sense of responsibility.

Chapter 15/Riding the Road Ahead

*...The beardless youth, his tutor being at
length dismissed, delights in horses, and dogs,
and the sunny expanse of the turf.*

—Horace

For more than a century, the Hearsts, at least some of them, have been in love with horses. The gold miner's great-grand-son George Hearst enjoys his horses on his own ranch near Ventura, California, and he actively participates in such rodeo-related horse sports as Team Roping and Steer Stopping. With his two sons, George and Stephen, he forms a team of three to enter competitive cowboy events, which are becoming very popular in California. In one, called Team Penning, three mounted riders in an arena attempt to take their assigned three head of steer out of a herd of thirty and move them into an enclosure at the far end of the arena. This requires expert riders and expert horses.

Young George, the great-great-grandson of George the miner, lives in San Francisco where he and his brother, Stephen, also play polo, a game in which, according to the players, "you have to ride like a Comanche, think like a chess player, and hit like a golf pro, while four players try to break your kneecaps." These young Hearsts and their sisters, Mary and Erin, spend many weekends riding at their father's Ventura ranch. Mary's two little girls, Shannon and Alexis, aged twelve and eleven—great-great-great-granddaughters of Senator George— both love to ride their two horses.

My husband, William, and his younger brother, Randolph, purchased some of the desert-bred Arabian horses when their father died. Randy subsequently sold his mares, although he now owns two Arabian riding horses, and a few years ago he decided to breed miniature Sicilian donkeys.

"What cute little animals," he enthused. "Why, they're not much bigger than dogs." He thought they would make perfect pets for his little girls, Catherine, Gina, Patty, Anne, and Vicky, What happened? Well, the girls grew up and the donkeys didn't. The girls, especially Jina, Patty, and Vicky, have continued to ride normal-sized horses,

Riding the Road Ahead by
Sam Savitt

In 1911 three-year-old
William Randolph
Hearst, Jr., learns to ride
at his grandmother
Phoebe's house.

but the tiny donkeys were retired to San Simeon Ranch, where they spent their old age in a front field on the highway, grazing with the cows, watching the cars go by.

Patty Hearst, who still rides a lot, carries on the traditional Hearst love affair with horses. She and her husband, Bernard Shaw (no relation to the playwright), have put the tragedy of her kidnapping behind them and concentrate their spare time and money on their two daughters. They planned to breed Welsh Ponies, Type B, but since moving to the East have put aside that dream.

Ancestors of the Pony of Wales of the British Isles are thought to have been domesticated in the Bronze Age, three-thousand years ago. Tenth-century documents mention herds of ponies living wild in the southern parts of England. The English stud book of Welsh ponies, begun in 1902, divides this ancient breed into sections. The smallest mountain pony is listed as Section A. Section B ponies must not exeed

13.2 hands in height and look like a small horse with beautiful action, whereas Section D, the Welsh cob type, averages 14 to 15 hands. Size aside, all of the types are animals of outstanding strength and action, and hardiness and endurance are bred into them. Whether large or small, they should have a small head, wide-set eyes, silky hair, small pricked ears, and a generous chest, and they may not be piebald or skewbald.

So the Welsh pony is the last of the many breeds to come to San Simeon. When our grandson, William Hearst, could hardly talk he was babbling about "pon-ee and cart," having ridden in the pony cart in Central Park when he visited us. So we have purchased an antique wicker governess cart, the harness, and a Welsh pony, Type B. She is officially known as SEMAIR SEREN #17932, a little grey mare sired by B-9838, LITTLE JOE II, out of BRYNTIRION SEREN, and bred at Semair Farm at Santa Barbara, California.

Grandmother bought George Hearst, Jr., and W.R. Hearst, Jr., a pony carriage with a pair of grays.

Willie's Welsh pony,
SEMAIR SERENE

She has pony-clubbed, and she jumps and drives like a perfect little lady. Safe as a foam-rubber playpen, she enjoys children; she likes their little hands rubbing her and she doesn't object to their climbing on and off her back and taking other liberties. "Seeweena" as our grandson calls her, was a family pet for the children of the last owners, the John Maddux family of Arroya Grande, California. They won many ribbons both riding and driving their Welsh mare.

What child hasn't prayed to God for a pony? As a child, I felt my own faith in God renewed because my prayers for a pony were answered, kind of, when a cousin of the family lent us a black pony for the summer. The happiness of your own real pony can never be forgotten. So our happy grandson has started his horse career, inherited from his father, his great-great-grandfather George, the miner, his great-grandfather William, the castle builder, and his grandfather, William, my husband. I hope for this little boy what Daphne Machin Goodall hopes

in her poem: "that horses will teach him their charity, their courage, kindness, and loyalty.

"Let him learn that this, this is one of God's noblest creatures."

So we come to the end of this book, which is a true love story—a story of love and perfect union between the Hearsts and their horses. And it ends with a look to the future, the beginning of another chapter, and with the age-old final words of every true love story: They lived happily ever after.

Mrs. William Randolph Hearst, Jr.

Appendix A: Races Won by George Hearst Horses

Matt Allen, *Trainer*

1888

April 21, SURINAM, O'Brien, Tidal Stakes, San Francisco, Bay District course

April 24, SURINAM, O'Brien, Pacific Derby, San Francisco

July 5, *GORGO, Littlefield, Free Handicap, Monmouth Park

August 4, SURINAM, Littlefield, Free Handicap, Monmouth Park

September 4, *GORGO, Littlefield, Siren Stakes, Sheepshead Bay

September 25, QUESTION, Sweepstakes, Gravesend

1889

April 30, MISS BELL, Armstrong, Purse, Memphis

May 8, BALLARAT, Hamilton, Hudson Stakes, Gravesend

June 22, BAGGAGE, Finnegan, $1000 Purse, Chicago, Washington Park

July 24, MISS BELL, Ellis, Purse, Minneapolis

July 26, MISS BELL, Taral, Purse, Minneapolis

July 27, MISS BELL, Ellis, Purse, Minneapolis

August 3, MISS BELL, Hamilton, $1,000 Purse, Morris Park

September 12, TOURNAMENT, Midgeley, Great Eastern Handicap, Sheepshead Bay

September 18, PHILANDER, Midgeley, Brooklyn Sweepstakes, Gravesend

September 20, TOURNAMENT, Covington, Holly Handicap, Gravesend

October 5, *GORGO, Hayward, Record Stakes, Morris Park

October 9, *GORGO, Hamilton, Handicap Sweepstakes, Morris Park

1890

April 5, *DEL MAR, Morton Sweepstakes, San José, California

June 5, GLOAMING, Covington, Elm Stakes, Morris Park

July 2, TOURNAMENT, Hayward, Realization, Sheepshead Bay

July 9, ALMONT, Narvice, Great Western Handicap, Chicago, Washington Park

July 10, *DEL MAR, Narvice, Purse, Chicago, Washington Park

July 19, ANARCHIST, Freeman, Purse, Chicago, Washington Park

July 24, ALMONT, Van Cleve, Purse, St. Paul, Minnesota.

Albert Cooper, *Trainer*

July 26, RHONO, Midgeley, Free Handicap, Monmouth Park

July 29, MISS BELL, Midgeley, Free Handicap Sweepstakes, Monmouth Park

July 31, RHONO, Midgeley, Adirondack Handicap, Saratoga

August 19, TOURNAMENT, Hayward, Omnibus Stakes, Monmouth Park

August 21, RHONO, Hamilton, Delaware Handicap, Monmouth Park

August 23, TOURNAMENT, Hayward, Choice Stakes, Monmouth Park

September 6, TOURNAMENT, Hayward, Omnium Handicap, Sheepshead Bay

September 26, RHONO, Hayward, Holly Handicap, Gravesend

October 1, TOURNAMENT, Hayward, Jerome Stakes, Morris Park

October 3, TOURNAMENT, Hayward, Mosholu Stakes, Morris Park

October 7, TOURNAMENT, Hayward, Hickory Stakes, Morris Park

October 11, TOURNAMENT, Hayward, New Rochelle Stakes, Morris Park

October 13, YOSEMITE, Decker, Sweepstakes, Morris Park

October 28, YOSEMITE, Thompson, Handicap, Linden Park, New Jersey

October 29, YOSEMITE, Lamley, Handicap Sweepstakes, Linden Park, New Jersey

November 1, YOSEMITE, J. Tribe, Handicap Sweepstakes, Linden Park, New Jersey

Appendix B: Piedra Blanca Broodmares

Broodmares purchased from *James Ben Ali Haggin,* **Rancho del Paso, Sacramento, with dates of their first foals for Hearst:**

BELLE S. by BAZAR
   1885—DOLLY S., bay filly by
   *KYRLE DALY

DAISY S. by LONGFIELD ex BELLE S.
   1889—bay colt by *CHEVIOT

SISTER TO LOTTERY by MONDAY
   1889—LORENA, bay filly
   by *CHEVIOT

SWEET PEGGY by *KYRLE DALY
   1889—BERNARDO, brown colt
   by *CHEVIOT

TRAMPO by *KYRLE DALY
   1890—BLIZZARD, bay colt by
   *TRADE WIND

MARIA F. by LEINSTER
   1891—bay colt by *CHEVIOT

EVERGLADE by IROQUOIS (purchased
   1887 as a racing prospect by
   Matt Allen)
   1892—black colt by JIM BROWN

Broodmares purchased from *Theodore Winters,* **El Arroyo Stud, Winters, California:**

NELLIE COLLIER by JOE HOOKER
   1886—WHY-NOT, chestnut filly by
   THREE CHEERS

ABBEY by NORFOLK
   1887—COSETTE, chestnut filly
   by JOE HOOKER

LAURA WINSTON by NORFOLK
   1889—barren, bred by JIM BROWN

CHESTNUT BELLE by NORFOLK
   1889—BIG BERTHA, chestnut
   filly by JIM BROWN

PROXIMATE by NORFOLK
   1893—chestnut colt by
   JIM BROWN

Broodmares purchased from *Leland Stanford,* **Palo Alto Stud, California**

*FUN by FIDDLER
   1890—chestnut filly by
   JIM BROWN

LENOKE by SHANNON
   1891—foal by JIM BROWN

Broodmares purchased from *Major Barak Thomas,* **Dixiana Stud, Lexington, Kentucky:**

VIOLA (IRENA) by HIMYAR
   1888—CHARLEY BROWN,
   chestnut colt by JIM BROWN

ELSIE BAN by *KING BAN
   1890—bay colt by JIM BROWN

MARY RUSSELL by *KING BAN
   1891—bay colt by *SAN SIMEON

Broodmares purchased from *A. J. Hutchinson,* **California:**

MERCEDES (VIVANDIÈRE) by LODI
   1889—MERCED, brown filly
   by *CHEVIOT

VIXEN by *SAXON
   1889—RAGNA, bay filly by
   JIM BROWN

EVELITH by HOCK HOCKING
   (purchased 1888 as racing
   prospect by Matt Allen)
   1892—black colt by JIM BROWN

Broodmares purchased from other sellers:

MISTLETOE by THAD STEVENS,
   purchased from *Dan N. Burns,*
   San Francisco
   1890—brown colt by *CHEVIOT

CARRIE C. by SCAMPERDOWN,
   (seller unknown)
   1889—GONZALEZ, bay colt by
   *CHEVIOT

DECEPTION by TEN BROECK,
   purchased from *C. D. Farrar,*
   South Carolina
   1892—CECIL, bay filly by
   JIM BROWN

MISS PICKWICK by *MR. PICKWICK,
   purchased from *Charles Reed,*
   Fairview Stud, Gallatin,
   Tennessee
   1893—bred to SURINAM

Broodmares imported from Australia by George Hearst:

*BEAUTY by THE DRUMMER, bred by
   F. Reynolds
   1889—DR. ROSS, brown colt by
   *CHEVIOT

*PALOMA by THE DRUMMER, bred by
   F. Reynolds
   1890—PALOMITA, chestnut filly
   by JIM BROWN

*VICTRESS by GOLDSBOROUGH, bred
   by W. J. Dangar
   1890—VICTORESS, chestnut filly
   by JIM BROWN

*BORBUS by *DAREBIN, bred by
   Andrew Towne
   1891—bay filly by *CHEVIOT

*MERRIMAC by GOLDSBOROUGH, bred by F. Reynolds
1891—foal by *CHEVIOT

*GERTRUDE by SOMNUS, bred by Andrew Towne; bought by Matt Allen as a racing prospect for Hearst
1893—chestnut filly by SURINAM

Broodmares bred by George Hearst:

LILLIE S, chestnut mare
1884 by LONGFIELD ex BELLE S.

DOLLY S., bay mare
1885 by *KYRLE DALY ex BELLE S.

MINNIEOLA, chestnut mare
1887 by WARWICK ex BELLE S.

EMMA COLLIER, chestnut mare
1887 by DUKE OF NORFOLK ex NELLIE COLLIER

COSETTE, chestnut mare
1887 by JOE HOOKER ex ABBEY by NORFOLK

CHIPPIE, chestnut mare
1888 by JIM BROWN ex DAISY S.

BIG BERTHA, chestnut mare
1889 by JIM BROWN ex CHESTNUT BELLE

EMMA H., bay mare
1889 by *CHEVIOT ex DOLLY S.

BERNA, bay mare
1890 by *CHEVIOT ex SWEET PEGGY

JENNIE H., bay mare
1889 by *CHEVIOT ex DOLLY S.

Appendix C: Piedra Blanca Stallions

*CHEVIOT

*CHEVIOT arrived at Piedra Blanca in 1888 and was bred to Hearst's mares. At the sales after George Hearst's death, the stallion's offspring sold for good prices and almost all had successful racing careers. *CHEVIOT, a bay horse bred by the Middle Park Stud Company in New Zealand, with his brother *SIR MODRED (owned by James Ben Ali Haggin), was proof of the good blood from down under.

JIM BROWN

Although *CHEVIOT was the premier stallion at Piedra Blanca, a California-bred horse was given an equal opportunity to prove his worth as a sire of racehorses. This was JIM BROWN, a chestnut colt foaled 1878, by FOSTER ex FLUSH by HIAWATHA, bred by W. L. Pritchard. In the November 20, 1891, dispersal sale the horse's racing career was summarized as follows:

JIM BROWN as a two-year-old started in five races, won two, and was second in another; one of his victories was in the Conner Stakes at Oakland, which he won over a very heavy track, beating FRANK RHOADS and the Hubbard-Demirep colt. As a three-year-old he won the Spirit of the Times Stake, mile and three-quarters, at Oakland, beating DUKE OF NORFOLK, FRED COLLIER and FRANK RHOADS in 3:06, and won a sweepstakes for three-year-olds, at Sacramento, mile and a half in 2:36, carrying proper weight and defeating FRED COLLIER, JIM DOUGLAS and WINIFRED; ran second to CLARA D. in a mile-and-three-quarter run, and was retired to the stud.

The following appeared in the July 19, 1893, sale catalogue of Piedra Blanca yearlings:

JIM BROWN has never been given the opportunities in the stud that his breeding and produce warrant, being unfortunate in location for several years (at J. B. Haggins' Rancho Del Paso), where imported stallions were given preference; his opportunities for service were limited. He was the sire of that good race mare LAURA GARDNER (the LITTLE ESPERANZA of her day), an honest, consistent performer that won at all distances. She won the Fame Stake as a three-year-old in 1887; done her two miles in 3:34 with 115 pounds up, beating a field of good horses. She also won at a mile-and-a-half several times. Her best race at this distance was 2:37$\frac{1}{2}$. She ran in three-quarter heats and mile heats during her three-year-old career. The next season she started twenty times, winning thirteen, from such horses as DAISY D., APPLAUSE, IDALENE COTTON, MOSES B., JOHN TREAT, a good lot in their day.

He also sired IDALENE COTTON, NINENA (who started twenty-one times, winning eleven as a three-year-old) NANCY, REWARD, and the two-year-old filly EULALIE, now running and winning in the East.

He also sired BAGATELLE, a high-class broodmare in the Del Paso stud. She was the dam of MORRISTOWN (by MILNER), who won as two-year-old, beating such horses as GREGORY, SUCCESSOR, WATERLOO, and others. Nearly every one of his produce have raced and won.

The stallion's location at Rancho del Paso was not, in fact, a disadvantage. Three of the winners by JIM BROWN cited above were bred by Haggin, namely NINENA (1884), NANCY (1885), and REWARD (1886). Two other winners from the 1884 crop, LAURA GARDNER and IDALENE COTTON, were bred by Theodore Winters and W. L. Pritchard respectively. Several of California's leading breeders retained for their broodmare bands fillies they had bred by JIM BROWN. These included Theodore Winters, J. B. Haggin, W. L. Pritchard, D. W. Burns, S. G. Reed, and others.

JIM BROWN was moved to Piedra Blanca, the stud farm of his owner, in order to make the season of 1887; George Hearst bred two foals dropped there in 1888, CHARLEY BROWN and CHIPPIE. JIM BROWN also sired winners for Piedra Blanca, such as RAGNA, a bay filly foaled 1889 ex VIXEN, and EULALIE, a chestnut filly foaled 1891 ex *FUN, who sold as a yearling at auction in New York for $1,000.

George Hearst and the Hearst estate, in fact, gave JIM BROWN every opportunity. From 1888 to 1893 twenty-seven of his foals were born at Piedra Blanca, one in 1888, three in 1889, five in 1890, eight in 1891, nine in 1892, and one in 1893. These were the produce of sixteen of the stud's best mares, including three imported from Australia. It was *CHEVIOT whose get drew headlines, but JIM BROWN sired sound and consistent racehorses whose winning kept the stable accounts in the black.

SURINAM

During the winter of 1887–88 trainer Matt Allen purchased from Theodore Winters for the racing stable of George Hearst the chestnut colt foaled 1885 named SURINAM. This was a beautifully bred colt by JOE HOOKER out of ADA by REVENUE.

When SURINAM was sold at auction for $3,600 in San Francisco, November 20, 1893, the catalogue described his racing record as follows:

SURINAM as a two-year-old, in two stakes races finished first, but was disqualified for fouling. In one, the California Annual, he ran a mile in 1:42$\frac{3}{4}$, but the race was given to SNOWDROP. However, there was no claim of foul in the Autumn Stake, one mile, which he captured in 1:44$\frac{1}{2}$, beating SNOWDROP, CANNY SCOTT, GERALDINE and BOLERO. He helped force out GERALDINE in 0:48$\frac{1}{4}$, the best time ever made for half a mile by a two-year-old on the Coast, and ran second in one other race.

Joseph Cairn Simpson, founder, publisher, and editor of the San Francisco-based weekly *The Breeder and Sportsman* in his issue of April 14, 1888, described Matt Allen's purchase as follows:

SURINAM has wintered well, and has grown in size and substance, so it is the more to be regretted that he was not entered in the Kentucky Derby. SURINAM last season was one of the best of our two-year-olds, but unfortunately, through foul riding, he was disqualified from two or three leading events in which he came in first.

The catalogue went on to describe his three-year-old form:

As a three-year-old SURINAM started five times, and won on three occasions. He placed to his credit the Tidal Stakes, 118 pounds up, mile and a quarter, over a heavy track in 2:13; won Pacific Derby, 119 lbs. up, mile and a half, in 2:38¼ easily, beating PEEL and five others. SURINAM was taken East and on his first appearance at Monmouth Park ran third to FIRENZI and EXILE in the Harvest Handicap, the three-year-old carrying 106 to FIRENZI's 118 as a four-year-old. Behind SURINAM were EURUS, CONNEMARA, PIRATE and FAVOR, all high-class stake horses. He next ran fourth in the Navesink Handicap, won by CONNEMARA in 2:35½, FIRENZI second, EURUS third. The winner, four years old, carried but 100 lbs., SURINAM, 3 years, 104 lbs. SURINAM wound up the racing season by winning a handicap sweepstakes at Monmouth, beating ARETINO, MONTAGE, CONNEMARA, GOANO, BOAZ, and THE BOURBON, 1¼ miles, in 2:09¾, carrying 105 lbs. to ARETINO's 98, he an aged horse. SURINAM was then sent to the stud, where he is proving a wonderful sire.

George Hearst gave SURINAM the opportunity to prove his worth as a sire. Five of his foals were born at Piedra Blanca in 1891. The young stallion was not included in the New York dispersal sale of May 14, 1891,

but was retained by the estate, for whom he sired another five foals in 1892, eight in 1893, and one in 1894.

The 1893 catalogue continues:

SURINAM must, in a spirit of fairness, be considered one of the best young sires in America. Three of his colts have appeared on the turf, and all have proved victorious. This is a grand showing, truly, especially when one of these is known to be ARMITAGE, winner of four straight races against the cracks of the East this season, and sold at auction to Richard Croker, of New York, for $8,000 considered to be less than half his true value.

*TRADE WIND and *TRUE BRITON

In 1888 Hearst had purchased as racing prospects two imported Australian horses, *TRADE WIND, a bay colt foaled 1885 (GOLDSBOROUGH—ROSEMARY) and *TRUE BRITON, a black colt foaled 1884 (JOHN BULL—RUBY). These were not included among the lots offered in the New York May 14, 1891, auction sale but were retained by the George Hearst estate and put to stud. *TRUE BRITON sired eight foals born in 1893, while *TRADE WIND was given even greater opportunities by Piedra Blanca. His get included two foals in 1890, one in 1891, two in 1892, and six in 1893. The November 20, 1893, catalogue in which *TRADE WIND was listed as Lot 3, noted that his 1890 bay colt BLIZZARD out of TRAMPO by *KYRLE DALY, had been a frequent winner in 1893.

KING THOMAS and *DEL MAR

The November 20, 1893, Piedra Blanca Stud dispersal sale catalogue lists thirty-five mares together with the names of the sires to which they had been bred that season. The stallions used in previous seasons

included SURINAM (eight mares), *TRUE BRITON (five mares), JIM BROWN (two mares), and *TRADE WIND and DR. ROSS (one mare each). Sires not previously used but moved to Piedra Blanca by the George Hearst estate for the 1893 season were KING THOMAS and *DEL MAR.

At the first Piedra Blanca dispersal sale, at the Sheepshead Bay track on May 14, 1891, KING THOMAS, the $40,000 yearling, was "knocked down" (for $4,000) to D. J. McCarty "who, it is whispered, acted for Trainer Albert Cooper [Hearst's trainer], who thinks that the big brother to BAN FOX and KING FOX is a racehorse." Since McCarty often represented the Hearst racing and breeding interests, it seems probable that the horse was actually bid in. At any rate he stood at Piedra Blanca in the spring of 1893 where he was bred to no less than fourteen mares.

The other sire added in 1893 to the Piedra Blanca stallion barn was the chestnut horse *DEL MAR, foaled in 1886, by *SOMNUS out of MAID OF THE HILLS, who was by the top Australian sire THE DRUMMER. As a four-year-old, *DEL MAR won three races at San José, Chicago, and St. Paul, Minnesota. In five out of eight starts at Sacramento, Oakland and Carson City, he won five races and was three times second. In 1893 he was bred to three mares at Piedra Blanca.

Bibliography

Albert, Paul. "Romance of the Western Stock Horse." *The Western Horseman* (April 1936).

Alexander, David. *The History and Romance of the Horse.* New York: Cooper Square Publishers, 1963.

The American Stud Book, Vol. VII. New York: The Jockey Club, 1898.

Angel, Myron. *History of San Luis Obispo County.* Berkeley, California: North Point Press, 1966.

Arnett, A.M. "Philip Henry Sheridan." *Encyclopaedia Britannica,* 1929 edition.

Barclay, Harold. *The Role of the Horse in Man's Culture.* London: J. A. Allen, 1980.

Battell, Joseph. *The Morgan Horse and Register,* Vol. I. Middlebury, Vermont: Register Printing Company, 1894.

Brown, William R. *The Horse of the Desert.* New York: Derry Dale Press, 1929.

Brunner, John. *Horses at Home.* London: Spring Books, n.d.

Burke, Carleton F. *The Thoroughbred of California Magazine,* March–May 1950.

Carter, W. T. *California Morgans of Yesterday: 20th Century Morgan Horse Directory.* Modesto, California: Northern California Morgan Horse Club, Inc., 1966.

Chapman, Arthur. *The Pony Express.* New York: G. P. Putnam's Sons, 1932.

Churchill, Peter, ed. *The World Atlas of Horses and Ponies.* New York: Crown Publishers, n.d.

Conkling, Roscoe P., and Margaret B. *The Butterfield Overland Mail 1857–1869.* Glendale, California: Arthur H. Clark Company, 1947.

Conn, George H. *The Arabian Horse in America.* Woodstock, Vermont: The Countryman Press, 1957.

Crowell, Pers. *Cavalcade of American Horses.* New York: McGraw-Hill Book Company, 1951.

Davenport, Homer. *My Quest of the Arabian Horse.* New York: B. W. Dodge & Company, 1909.

Denhardt, Robert Moorman. *The Horse of the Americas.* Norman, Oklahoma: University of Oklahoma Press, 1947.

Denhardt, Robert. *The Quarter Running Horse: America's Oldest Breed.* Athens, Ohio: Ohio University Press, 1979.

De Quille, Dan. *History of the Big Bonanza.* Hartford, Connecticut: American Publishing Company, 1877.

Disston, Harry. *Know About Horses.* New York: Devin-Adair Company, 1961.

Dunbar, Seymour. *The History of Travel in America.* Indianapolis: Bobbs Merrill Company, 1915.

Dunlop, Richard. *Wheels West.* Chicago: Rand McNally, 1977.

Dwyer, F. *Seats and Saddles, Bits and Bitting, Draught and Harness.* London: Wittingham, 1886.

Edwards, Elwyn H. ed. *Encyclopedia of the Horse.* New York: Crown Publishers, n.d.

Eldredge, Zoeth Skinner. *History of California,* Vol. I. New York: Century History Company, 1915.

Foster, Lee. *Adventures in California Country.* Beaverton, Oregon: Beautiful America Publishing Company, 1981.

Freeman, Douglas. "Little Sorrel." *Richmond News-Leader* (1939).

Gleason, Duncan. *The Islands and Ports of California.* New York: Devin-Adair Company, 1958.

Glyn, Richard. *The World's Finest Horses and Ponies.* Garden City, New York: Doubleday and Company, 1958.

Goodall, Daphne Machin. *Horses of the World.* New York: Macmillan and Company, 1965.

Goodwin, Cardinal. *Trans Mississippi West 1803–1853.* New York: publisher unknown, 1922.

Greeley, Horace. *Overland Journey.* New York: publisher unknown, 1860.

Gudde, Erwin G. *California Place Names.* Berkeley, California: University of California Press, 1962.

Hafen, LeRoy. *The Overland Mail 1849–1869.* Glendale, California: Arthur H. Clark Company, 1926.

Haines, Francis. *Appaloosa: The Spotted Horse in Art and History.* Austin, Texas: University of Texas Press, 1963.

Hamilton, Geneva. *Where the Highway Ends: Cambria, San Simeon and the Rancho.* San Luis Obispo, California: Padre Productions, 1974.

Harris, Albert W. *The Arabian Horses of Kemah.* Booklet. Lake Geneva, Wisconsin: Kemah Horse Farm, 1922.

———. *The Blood of the Arabs.* Chicago: Arabian Horse Clubs Registry of America, n.d.

Hollen, W. Eugene. *Great Days of the Overland Stage.* New York: American Heritage, 1957.

Houlton, La Vonne. *California Morgans of Yesterday: 19th Century Morgan Horse Directory.* Modesto, California: Northern California Morgan Horse Club, Inc., 1966.

Hoover, Mildred Brook; Rensch, Hero E.; and Rensch, Ethel G. *Historic Spots in California.* Stanford, California: Stanford University Press, 1932.

Hunt, Frazier and Robert. *Horses and Heroes.* New York: Charles Scribner's Sons, 1949.

Johnson, James Ralph, and Alfred, Hoyt Bill. *Horsemen, Blue and Grey.* New York: Oxford University Press, 1960

Laune, Paul. *America's Quarter Horses.* Garden City, New York: Doubleday and Company, 1973.

Lea, Tom. *The King Ranch*. Boston: publisher unknown, 1957.

Lewis, Paul. *Beautiful California Coast*. Beaverton, Oregon: Beautiful America Publishing Company, 1979.

Littauer, Vladimir. *Horsemen's Progress: The Development of Modern Riding*. New York: D. Van Nostrand Company, 1962.

Marryat, Frank. *Mountains and Molehills, or Recollections of a Burnt Journal*. London: Longmans, 1855.

McDonald, Douglas. *Virginia City and the Silver Region of the Comstock Lode*. Las Vegas: Nevada Publications, 1982.

McGroarty, Mr. *California, Its History and Romance*. Los Angeles: Grafton Publishing Company, 1911.

Mellin, Jeanne. *The Morgan Horse*. Brattleboro, Vermont: The Stephen Green Press, n.d.

Moody, Ralph. *Stagecoach West*. New York: Thomas Y. Crowell Company, 1967.

Moore, Dan. *Shoot Me a Biscuit: Log of a Twentieth Century Cowboy*. Tucson, Arizona: University of Arizona Press, 1974.

Morrison, Anne. *History of San Luis Obispo County*. Los Angeles: Los Angeles Historic Record Company, 1917.

Neider, Charles. *The Great West*. New York: Coward-McCann, 1958.

Nicholson, Loren. *Rails Across the Ranchos*. Fresno, California: Valley Publishers, 1980.

Norton, D. M. *The Palomino Horse*. Los Angeles: Borden Publishing Company, 1949.

Older, Mr. and Mrs. Fremont. *Life of George Hearst, California Pioneer, and Life of Phoebe Hearst*. Privately published, 1933.

Outland, Charles. *Stage Coaching on the Camino Real: Los Angeles to San Francisco 1861–1901*. Publisher unknown.

Patten, John W. *The Light Horse Breeds*. New York: A. S. Barnes and Company, 1960.

Pitt, Leonard. *The Decline of the Californios*. Berkeley, California: University of California Press, 1970.

Pittenger, Peggy Jett. *Morgan Horses*. New York: A. S. Barnes, n.d.

Phillips, Lance. *The American Saddle Horse*. New York: A. S. Barnes, 1984.

Reese, Herbert H. *Arabian Horse Breeding*. Los Angeles: Borden Publishing Company, 1953.

Riesenberg, Felix. *The Golden Road: The Story of California's Spanish Mission Trail*. New York: McGraw-Hill Book Company, 1962.

Rollins, Philip A. *The Cowboy*. New York: Ballantine Books, 1973.

Root and Connelley. *The Overland Stage to California*. Topeka, Kansas: publisher unknown, 1901.

Salley, Harold E. *History of California Post Offices 1849–1976*. Spring Valley, California: Heartland Printing and Publishing Company, 1977.

Saunders, Charles Francis, and Chase, J. Smeaton. *The California Padres and Their Missions*. Boston: Houghton Mifflin Company, 1960.

Savitt, Sam. *America's Horses*. Garden City, New York: Doubleday and Company, 1966.

Self, Margaret Cabell. *The American Horse Show*. New York: A. S. Barnes , 1958.

Selzer, Judy. "The San Simeon Endurance Ride," *Saddle Action Magazine* (November–December 1976).

Sierra Club, Santa Lucia Chapter. *San Luis Obispo County Trail Guide*. Booklet. San Luis Obispo, California, 1982.

Smythe, R. H. *The Mind of the Horse*. Brattleboro, Vermont: The Stephen Greene Press, 1966.

Strong, Phil. *Horses and Americas*. New York: Frederick Stokes, 1939.

Summer-Hays, R. S. *The Observer's Book of Horses and Ponies*. New York: Frederick Warne and Company, 1961.

Taylor, Lewis. *The Horse America Made*. New York: Harper and Brothers, 1961.

Thwaites, Jeanne. *Horses of the West*. New York: A. S. Barnes, 1968.

Van Nostrand, Jeanne. *A Pictorial and Narrative History of Monterey: Adobe Capital of California 1770–1847*. San Francisco: California Historical Society, 1968.

Vesey, Fitzgerald, ed. *The Book of the Horse*. London: Nicholson and Watson, 1946.

Wentworth, Lady. *Arabian Type and Standard*. London: William Collins, n.d.

————. *Authentic Arabian Horses and Descendants*. London: William Collins, n.d.

————. *Thoroughbred Racing Stock*. London: George Allen and Unwin, 1938.

Wieman, Harold. *Nature Walks on the San Luis Coast*. San Luis Obispo, California: Padre Productions, 1980.

Williamson, Ray A. *Living the Sky: The Cosmos of the American Indian*. Boston: Houghton Mifflin, 1984.

Wilson, J. G., and Fiske, J. *Appleton's Cyclopaedia of American Biography*. New York: publisher unknown, 1887–89.

Winslow, Carleton M. *Discovering San Luis Obispo County*. San Luis Obispo, California: privately published, 1972.

Winther, Oscar Osburn. *The Transportation Frontier: Trans Mississippi West 1865–1890*. New York: Holt, Rinehart and Winston, 1964.

Subject Index

Picture Credits

All photographs and illustrations not credited below have been reproduced from originals in the possession of the Hearst family.

Acknowledgments

In preparing this book I have been fortunate to receive assistance, information, and support from many individuals and institutions.

I am especially grateful to each of the following for their advice and for making corrections in the various breed chapters: Darrell Dodds of *Appaloosa News;* Robert Dallmeyer, Secretary-Treasurer of the Palomino Horse Association; Jack Anderson, Past President, Earl Harper, General Manager, and Robert J. Shiflet, Executive Vice President of the Palomino Horse Breeders Association; Mrs. LaVonne Houlton, longtime breeder of Morgan horses; Richard Quattlander, American Morgan Horse Association; and Lynn Buxton Beckford, North American Morab Horse Association.

For research, I would like to acknowledge the assistance of Mrs. Mildred Wright, Picture Collection, and Donald Anderle, Associate Director for Special Collections, The New York Public Library; Lawrence Dinnean, Curator of Pictorial Collections, The Bancroft Library, University of California at Berkeley, and Dr. James Hart, Director of The Bancroft Library; T. G. Kay and Sheila Huloss of The British Library, London; Mary E. Genett, Assistant Librarian for Reference Services, the American Museum of Natural History, New York; the librarians of the California Polytechnic State University Library, San Luis Obispo; the Fine Arts Museums of San Francisco; Janet Peterson of World Books Encyclopedia; Professor Woodson Frey, Ornamental Horticulture Department, California Polytechnic State University.

For lending pictures and for permitting me to reproduce them, I am grateful to the following: Miss Courtney Hoyt of Life Picture Service; Rob Ness; Dan Heath of Nevada Western Gallery; Mr. and Mrs. Harlan Brown; LaVonne Houlton; Kay Lynn Sherman; Peggy Yeyna of *The Cambrian;* Frank Hyatt of Wide World Photos; Richard and Kathe Tanner; Mrs. Elvira Kiehlbauch; Sam Harris; Ken Murray; Jack Cooke and Phoebe Hearst Cooke; Charlotte Olmstead of Sunset Books; Andrea K. Juricic; Sandra Buchman of the Department of Parks and Recreation, State of California; Mr. and Mrs. James Williams; Donald Brenson of *Saddle Action Magazine;* Raymond Levering; Lavoux Studio, and the Princes of Liechtenstein.

It is with special gratitude that I acknowledge the considerable contributions of these individuals:

Sam Savitt, for encouraging me at every stage, and for pushing and guiding me through the years of study and research. Sam found the printer for this book and he also suggested Alexander Mackay-Smith, who contributed much research, many ideas, and a number of important corrections, as well as the foreword. Sam also led me to Barbara Burn, who edited the final manuscript; Barbara in turn introduced Michael Shroyer, who designed the book, and Alix Coleman, who took the wonderful photographs especially for the project. I am endlessly grateful to each of them, but above all to Sam for his inspiring pictures and to Bette Savitt for always helping Sam; Bob Reynolds, for his handsome paintings and for arranging numerous trips so that I could obtain photographs of maps and paintings at San Simeon; Taylor Coffman and Peter and Louise Sebastian, for contributing data about the early history of the Hearst ranch; and, last but not least, Dorothy Bitetto, Anne Cremarosa, Nancy Gallegos, Inge-Britt Johansson, Helen Kurtz, Kim Parker, Mildred Schindler, Delcine Stevenson, and Rosemary Ziegler, who all helped with research, filing, typing, copying, checking haphazard spelling, finding lost items, making and answering telephone calls, writing checks, smiling at trouble, and administering soothing words to a crazed author.